Urban Sprawl

Other Books in the Current Controversies Series

Urban Sprawl

Noël Merino, Book Editor

GREENHAVEN PRESS
A part of Gale, Cengage Learning

GALE
CENGAGE Learning·

Detroit • New York • San Francisco • New Haven, Conn • Waterville, Maine • London

Elizabeth Des Chenes, *Director, Content Strategy*
Cynthia Sanner, *Publisher*
Douglas Dentino, *Manager, New Product*

© 2014 Greenhaven Press, a part of Gale, Cengage Learning

WCN: 01-100-101

LIBRARY OF CONGRESS CATALOGING-IN-PUBLICATION DATA

Urban sprawl / Noël Merino, book editor.
    p. cm. -- (Current controversies)
    Includes bibliographical references and index.
    ISBN 978-0-7377-6247-1 (hardcover) -- ISBN 978-0-7377-6248-8 (pbk.)
    1. Cities and towns--Growth. 2. City planning--Environmental aspects. 3. Land use, Urban. I. Merino, Noël, editor of compilation.
    HT371.U7296 2014
    307.76--dc23
                                      2013033391

Printed in the United States of America
1 2 3 4 5 6 7 18 17 16 15 14

Contents

Cities built for cars instead of people lead to poor health outcomes, but the problem can be addressed by policy decisions that make it easier for people to walk or cycle to work and other destinations, and make driving a car less attractive.

No: Urban Sprawl Is Not a Serious Problem

Urban sprawl has been a feature of cities throughout history and automobiles are merely one in a series of new technologies, such as the railroad and the horse drawn carriage, that allowed people to escape the congestion and health hazards of urban centers. In reality, transportation by automobile in decentralized regions is more efficient and, today, less poluting than travel by mass transit in high-density urban cities. Thus, the focus of planners and government officials should not be to force people into outmoded forms of transportation but to encourage the development of new fuel sources and new types of transport to serve both large cities and suburban areas.

Chapter 2: Does Urban Sprawl Harm the Environment?

Kaid Benfield

With America's population expected to increase by seventy million people in the next twenty-five years, we must invest in the country's existing cities and suburbs to absorb the expected growth, not continue to develop rural land and increase urban sprawl. Only in this way can we save the environment and ensure the health of our planet.

David Owen, interviewed by Jared Green

Dense urban centers are more environmentally sustainable than the suburbs because city dwellers drive less, live closer to work and other destinations, share public space, and don't own individual yards to maintain. In fact, New York City has the lowest per capita use of energy than anywhere else in America.

Josh Harkinson

Opposition to infill development that promotes urban density, even by environmentalists, is misguided and often disingenuous. Urbanites and environmental groups—many of whom support sustainable projects—must learn to overcome the "not in my backyard" mentality when it comes to such infill development or risk marginalizing their ideas.

No: Urban Sprawl Does Not Harm the Environment

Chapter 3: What Effect Does Urban Sprawl Have on the Economy?

Although the economic recession has caused urban sprawl to slow, those who predict the end of suburbia fail to account for the enduring appeal of home ownership and automobile travel—qualities that will continue to make suburban living attractive to consumers.

Affordable housing that is subsidized for low-income families is often built far away from public transit, schools, and jobs, thereby increasing transportation costs and making these homes much less affordable than they seem. Building affordable housing close to transportation systems and within walking distance of most necessities, including employment, is the best way to help low-income people.

Chapter 4: How Should Urban Sprawl Be Managed?

Foreword

By definition, controversies are "discussions of questions in which opposing opinions clash" (*Webster's Twentieth Century Dictionary Unabridged*). Few would deny that controversies are a pervasive part of the human condition and exist on virtually every level of human enterprise. Controversies transpire between individuals and among groups, within nations and between nations. Controversies supply the grist necessary for progress by providing challenges and challengers to the status quo. They also create atmospheres where strife and warfare can flourish. A world without controversies would be a peaceful world; but it also would be, by and large, static and prosaic.

The Series' Purpose

The purpose of the Current Controversies series is to explore many of the social, political, and economic controversies dominating the national and international scenes today. Titles selected for inclusion in the series are highly focused and specific. For example, from the larger category of criminal justice, Current Controversies deals with specific topics such as police brutality, gun control, white collar crime, and others. The debates in Current Controversies also are presented in a useful, timeless fashion. Articles and book excerpts included in each title are selected if they contribute valuable, long-range ideas to the overall debate. And wherever possible, current information is enhanced with historical documents and other relevant materials. Thus, while individual titles are current in focus, every effort is made to ensure that they will not become quickly outdated. Books in the Current Controversies series will remain important resources for librarians, teachers, and students for many years.

In addition to keeping the titles focused and specific, great care is taken in the editorial format of each book in the series. Book introductions and chapter prefaces are offered to provide background material for readers. Chapters are organized around several key questions that are answered with diverse opinions representing all points on the political spectrum. Materials in each chapter include opinions in which authors clearly disagree as well as alternative opinions in which authors may agree on a broader issue but disagree on the possible solutions. In this way, the content of each volume in Current Controversies mirrors the mosaic of opinions encountered in society. Readers will quickly realize that there are many viable answers to these complex issues. By questioning each author's conclusions, students and casual readers can begin to develop the critical thinking skills so important to evaluating opinionated material.

Current Controversies is also ideal for controlled research. Each anthology in the series is composed of primary sources taken from a wide gamut of informational categories including periodicals, newspapers, books, US and foreign government documents, and the publications of private and public organizations. Readers will find factual support for reports, debates, and research papers covering all areas of important issues. In addition, an annotated table of contents, an index, a book and periodical bibliography, and a list of organizations to contact are included in each book to expedite further research.

Perhaps more than ever before in history, people are confronted with diverse and contradictory information. During the Persian Gulf War, for example, the public was not only treated to minute-to-minute coverage of the war, it was also inundated with critiques of the coverage and countless analyses of the factors motivating US involvement. Being able to sort through the plethora of opinions accompanying today's major issues, and to draw one's own conclusions, can be a complicated and frustrating struggle. It is the editors' hope that Current Controversies will help readers with this struggle.

Introduction

> *"The debate about the impact of sprawl on transportation choices, and the extent to which government policy should intervene, is just one of the many controversies about development outside the urban core."*

Hope Yen and Kristen Wyatt of the Associated Press reported recently, "For the first time in a century, most of America's largest cities are growing at a faster rate than their surrounding suburbs."[1] The economic recession is cited as one of the causes of the trend, since young people "are delaying careers, marriage and having children amid persistently high unemployment." In conjunction with this trend is a shift among young people away from automobiles in favor of walking, biking, and public transportation. A recent study noted, "From 2001 to 2009, the average annual number of vehicle-miles traveled by young people (16- to 34-year-olds) decreased from 10,300 miles to 7,900 miles per capita—a drop of 23 percent."[2] The authors attribute this trend to changing preferences: "Many of America's youth prefer to live places where they can easily walk, bike, and take public transportation." Whether this trend continues remains to be seen, but what it does illustrate is the close connection between sprawl and transportation choices.

---

1. Hope Yen and Kristen Wyatt, "Cities Grow More than Suburbs, First Time in 100 Years," *Today*, June 28, 2012. http://today.msnbc.msn.com/id/47992439/ns/today -money/t/cities-grow-more-suburbs-first-time-years.

2. Benjamin Davis, Tony Dutzik, and Phineas Baxandall, "Transportation and the New Generation: Why Young People Are Driving Less and What It Means for Transportation Policy," Frontier Group and US PIRG Education Fund, April 2012. http:// www.uspirg.org/sites/pirg/files/reports/Transportation%20%26%20the%20New% 20Generation%20vUS_0.pdf.

Critics of suburban and exurban development claim that this sprawl has created many transportation-based problems. One critic noted that for those who do not have a car, choices are few and far between: "In suburbia, public transportation is rare or nonexistent."[3] Another noted how suburban design has limited transportation options by discouraging walking and biking: "We have, in effect, made getting around by foot or bicycle the most dangerous and least attractive option, though some brave souls risk their safety to walk or bicycle despite the hostility of the environment."[4]

Shortly after taking office President Barack Obama indicated that his administration would focus on policy that increases mass transit and moves away from supporting sprawl: "I would like for us to invest in mass transit. . . . I think people are a lot more open now to thinking regionally, in terms of how we plan our transportation infrastructure. The days where we're just building sprawl forever, those days are over."[5] Shortly thereafter the US Department of Housing and Urban Development (HUD) and US Department of Transportation (DOT) announced their plans for promoting sustainable communities in order to give American families "more choices for affordable housing near employment opportunities; more transportation options, to lower transportation costs, shorten travel times, and improve the environment; and safe, livable, healthy communities."[6]

3. Vanessa Quirk, "Saving Suburbia Part I: Bursting the Bubble," *ArchDaily*, April 26, 2012. http://www.archdaily.com/229385/saving-suburbia-part-i-bursting-the-bubble.

4. Kaid Benfield, "The True Cost of Unwalkable Streets," *Atlantic Cities*, March 28, 2012. http://www.theatlanticcities.com/commute/2012/03/true-cost-unwalkable-streets/1616.

5. Barack Obama, "Remarks by the President at Fort Myers Town Hall," White House, Office of the Press Secretary, February 10, 2009. http://www.whitehouse.gov/the_press_office/Remarks-by-the-President-at-Fort-Myers-Town-Hall.

6. Melanie Roussell, "HUD and DOT Announce Interagency Partnership to Promote Sustainable Communities," US Department of Housing and Urban Development, March 18, 2009. http://portal.hud.gov/hudportal/HUD?src=/press/press_releases_media_advisories/2009/HUDNo. 09-023.

This policy change of the Obama administration did not go over well with many Americans. One critic claims that it constitutes an antisuburban bias: "Today, approximately 75 percent of Americans live in the suburbs. . . . Despite these near-universal preferences, however, many liberals continue to oppose the trend of suburbanization."[7] Another worries that the attempt to limit sprawl is classist. "Intentionally or not, the War on Sprawl is a war on the working class," claims one critic of restrictions on sprawl, worrying that limits on suburban development will hurt the poor the most: "The real question is not whether we sprawl but who gets the benefits of single-family homeownership and automobility."[8] Even proponents of urban development over suburban development note, "Suburbanites *like* the suburbs. To dismiss the deeply ingrained desire for a buffer zone between one household and another is to turn potential allies into a hostile cul-de-sac army."[9]

The debate about the impact of sprawl on transportation choices, and the extent to which government policy should intervene, is just one of the many controversies about development outside the urban core. The debate about sprawl starts from the first premise: Is urban sprawl a problem at all? A frequent area of debate is urban sprawl's impact on the environment, with those who argue that dense city living is better for the environment and those who deny any environmental fallout from suburban living. The decline in suburban living during the recession seems to indicate that economic factors can influence the tendency to sprawl, but conflict abounds concerning the economic impact of sprawl. As we see with the

---

7. Ronald D. Utt, "President Obama's New Plan to Decide Where Americans Live and How They Travel," *Backgrounder*, April 14, 2009. http://www.heritage.org/research/reports/2009/04/president-obamas-new-plan-to-decide-where-americans-live-and-how-they-travel.

8. Randall O'Toole, "The War on the Working Class," *Oregon Catalyst*, March 26, 2012. http://oregoncatalyst.com/15877-war-working-class.html.

9. Justin Davidson, "Can This Suburb Be Saved?" *New York Magazine*, February 12, 2012. http://nymag.com/arts/architecture/reviews/foreclosed-suburb-davidson-2012-2.

Obama administration's proposal identified above, there is also wide disagreement about policies that attempt to manage sprawl. By exploring a wide variety of viewpoints, *Current Controversies: Urban Sprawl* attempts to illuminate some of the most current debates about urban sprawl.

CHAPTER 1

Is Urban Sprawl a Serious Problem?

Overview: Urban Sprawl in America

Haya El Nasser and Paul Overberg

Haya El Nasser is a demographics reporter and Paul Overberg a database editor at USA Today.

America's romance with sprawl may not be completely over, but it's definitely on the rocks.

Almost three years after the official end of a recession that kept people from moving and devastated new suburban subdivisions, people continue to avoid counties on the farthest edge of metropolitan areas, according to Census estimates out today [April 5, 2012].

Growth in Metro Areas

The financial and foreclosure crisis forced more people to rent. Soaring gas prices made long commutes less appealing. And high unemployment drew more people to big job centers. As the nation crawls out of the downturn, cities and older suburbs are leading the way.

Population growth in fringe counties nearly screeched to a halt in the year that ended July 1, 2011. By comparison, counties at the core of metro areas are growing faster than the nation as a whole.

"There's a pall being cast on the outer edges," says John McIlwain, senior fellow for housing at the Urban Land Institute, a non-profit development group that promotes sustainability. "The foreclosures, the vacancies, the uncompleted roads. It's uncomfortable out there. The glitz is off."

A *USA TODAY* analysis shows:

- All but two of the 39 counties with 1 million-plus people—Michigan's Wayne (Detroit) and Ohio's Cuyahoga (Cleveland)—grew from 2010 to 2011.

- Twenty-eight of the big counties gained faster than the nation, which grew at the slowest rate since the Great Depression (0.73%). The counties' median growth rate was 1.3% (half grew faster, half slower).

Those 28—including California's Alameda and Contra Costa counties, Florida's Broward and Hillsborough, Texas' Harris and Dallas—generated more than a third of the USA's growth. Before the recession and housing bust, when people flocked to new development on farmland, they contributed just 27%.

"It shows the locational advantage of being in the biggest cities," says Robert Lang, professor of urban affairs at the University of Nevada-Las Vegas and author of *Megapolitan America*. "The core is what's left of our competitiveness as a country."

Central metro counties accounted for 94% of U.S. growth, compared with 85% just before the recession.

Aging Baby Boomers, who have begun to retire, and Millennials, who are mostly in their teens and 20s, are more inclined to live in urban areas.

The End of Sprawl

"This could be the end of the exurb as a place where people aspire to go when they're starting their families," says William Frey, demographer at the Brookings Institution. "So many people have been burned by this. . . . First-time home buyers, immigrants and minorities took a real big hit."

During the '70s gas shortage and the '80s savings and loan industry crisis, some predicted the end of suburban sprawl. It didn't happen then, but current trends could change the nation's growth patterns permanently.

Aging Baby Boomers, who have begun to retire, and Millennials, who are mostly in their teens and 20s, are more inclined to live in urban areas, McIlwain says.

"I'm not sure we're going to see outward sprawl even if the urge to sprawl continues," he says. "Counties are getting to the point that they don't have the money to maintain the roads, water, sewer. . . . This is a century of urbanization."

Maybe, Lang says, "sprawl is the Freddy Krueger of American development. It's always pronounced dead and yet somehow springs back to life."

Urban Sprawl Is a Problem

Kevin Klinkenberg

Kevin Klinkenberg is a senior planner for an engineering and design firm and the author of NewUrbanismBlog.com.

One of the downsides of our modern world of communication is that contrary voices are often given equal weight and airtime, whether they deserve it or not. Media is so eager to present "the other side" that nearly anyone can trot out an opinion and give it some amount of credence, even when it's absurd. The challenge then is—do you respond? Do those of us who know better bother to give our time to someone who is so obviously wrong about an issue?

I thought about this as I listened to Robert Bruegmann speak last night at the Savannah College of Art and Design (SCAD), giving his lecture titled, "Sprawl: Learning to love it or at least think twice about trying to stop it." Bruegmann's title is provocative on purpose, as he promotes a book that he published in 2005. His lecture was rife with so many inaccuracies, cherry-picked statistics and flawed assumptions that, by his own admission, it tends to anger people. With about 200 people in attendance, mostly students, I feel it's too important not to respond.

The Definition of Sprawl

Since Bruegmann is being provocative on purpose, I feel no remorse for calling much of what he promotes as misleading at best, blatant lies at worst. As I said following the lecture, I almost don't know where to begin.

And so, I'll begin with how he defines sprawl. Like many people who rely on statistics, Bruegmann lumps all urban expansion of the last 150 years together as the same thing, as if there's no material difference between the streetcar suburbs of the 19th century and post-WWII automobile-dependent suburbs. Sadly, though, Bruegmann teaches in an architecture school, so he should know better. But for those who don't, let me reiterate a basic point—*all urban expansion is not sprawl.*

There is a fundamental difference between how cities expanded in the 19th through the early 20th century, and how they have expanded since. In the former, cities expanded as a series of connected neighborhoods. They were arranged on streets designed for walking, riding a bicycle and even had access to quality public transportation. Yes, they were lower density and more spacious than the city centers that they were attached to, but they were fundamentally walkable neighborhoods. Since the end of WWII, cities around the world, but most especially American cities, have expanded as a disconnected set of subdivisions, shopping centers and offices, only held together by a network of car sewers. This is not a minor difference—the two patterns of development are qualitatively and quantitatively different in every respect. Understanding this is Urban Planning 101. Equating all urban expansion as sprawl is a fundamental error underlying this book and lecture.

Brueggman then presents us with a series of statistics to show the shocking idea that as people become wealthier they tend to want a little more space, and even single family houses. Well, duh. Those of us who are New Urbanists or critics of sprawl would never argue otherwise. Single family houses do not equate to sprawl. Car ownership does not equate to sprawl. This is the point of decades of critique—it's not about all the pieces that make up our cities' growth areas, it's about how they are arranged. He argues we are "forcing people to live another way"—an often parroted critique of urban planners. I must say, it gets really old to mention that the whole system today in virtually every city and town in the US, whether it's zoning, lending standards, transportation planning, construction techniques, etc etc is all set up to produce sprawl. But really, shouldn't a professional in the field know this?

To say that sprawl is not a problem is not only untrue, it's destructive.

I feel that I could go on for pages regarding the foolishness of these arguments and the inaccuracies. But in order not to bore you, the reader, here's a quick summary of some other points:

- His critique that all the planning Portland, OR has done hasn't changed travel patterns or lifestyle is another lie from the playbook of Randall O'Toole. Fortunately, this was debunked years ago by Michael Lewyn.

- He stated that building in a denser fashion "might be more efficient economically." Um—here's the truth. It IS more efficient. On a per unit basis (the only metric that matters), it is unequivocal. Ever wonder why developers want to squeeze more units in?

- Not surprisingly, he minimized the threat of Peak Oil. Well, I suppose it's also possible that gravity is still a theory, but I wouldn't hedge my bets on it. Finite resources are just that—finite.

- He frequently cites European sprawl (and sometimes Asian) as examples that this phenomenon is everywhere, and that it is the same as in the U.S. Yes, other countries have their sprawl, too. But to say it works the same or is on the same scale as the U.S. is patently absurd. Many of those European suburbs are still walkable, and the actual amount that is auto-dependent is infinitesimal compared to American cities.

- He argues that buses as less efficient and worse for the environment because they get worse gas mileage and are typically under-utilized. Well, yes, buses in this country largely run under-used, but it's BECAUSE we've built places that make it difficult at best to ride a bus, if not impossible. In debate, they call this a straw man. And is there even a point to mentioning that buses can (and often do) run on alternative fuels?

- Like many sprawl apologists, he equated car usage with freedom of mobility. I like to equate freedom with having choices. In this case, choices include not only driving, but also walking, biking, or even taking transit. Anything less is dependence, not freedom.

The Importance of the Issue

I appreciate a good debate & intellectual challenge as much as anyone. And, I agree with Brueggman that many professionals tend to look down their noses at the suburbs and suburban expansion. And I would even go so far as to say that this can be a fascinating topic for debate—the question of "what to do about it" is one that divides us into many different camps professionally.

But to say that sprawl is not a problem is not only untrue, it's destructive. The environmental and economic consequences of our development patterns are proven facts. The social aspects are debatable, but they are real. Aesthetic critiques can be snobbery, but beauty does matter—human beings always gravitate toward it.

What I'm most left with after this lecture is the question of how can someone be a professional in the field of planning/architecture and deny the importance of this issue? It strikes me as no different than being a climate scientist and saying climate change is really no big deal, or being a health professional and poo-poohing the obesity epidemic. Yes, repairing sprawl may not be as important to humanity as feeding the poor or securing clean water for all, but within our profession it's the most important issue of our time.

Contrary views are very important to advancing intelligence and understanding. But sometimes they are just contrarian for the sake of being contrarian. That's not debate—that's either self-promotion or masturbation.

Urban Sprawl Drains Cities of Wealth

Gregory A. Galluzzo

Gregory A. Galluzzo, a former Jesuit priest, is the national direc-
tor and cofounder of the Gamaliel Foundation, a community-
organizing network.

I have been a community organizer in the tradition of Saul
Alinsky since 1972. I must confess that I regard my first 15
years of organizing as "cleaning the engine room of the Ti-
tanic." Working within the most unglamorous part of the
ship—the slums, the ghettos, and the barrios of America—we
focused on cleaning the grease, polishing the knobs, and adjusting the nozzles. In other words, we worked on getting rid
of drug houses, improving a park, and opening a health clinic,
while the ship itself was being steered "right" and towards certain disaster, rendering irrelevant all of our efforts in turning
communities around. To illustrate the point, I like to tell a
story.

The Parable of the Inner City

There once lived a people in a mountain valley with a beautiful lake at its center. The lake supported a diversity of wild
plant and animal life and was a source of recreation for the
valley's inhabitants. Water from the lake was used to create
beautiful fountains and to irrigate farms and gardens, as well
as to raise livestock. The well being of the valley and its inhabitants was totally dependent on the lake.

However, some people living in a valley below were very
jealous of the lifestyle enjoyed by the inhabitants of the upper

Gregory A. Galluzzo, "Organizing Against Urban Sprawl: A New Model," *Race, Poverty,
and the Environment*, vol. 15, no. 1, Fall 2008, pp. 13–15. Copyright © 2008 by Gregory
A. Galluzzo. All rights reserved. Reproduced by permission.

valley. So, they secretly dug a tunnel below the lake and proceeded to drain its water for their own purposes.

The people in the upper valley soon began to suffer. Their plant and animal life diminished and died, as did their crops and livestock. The fountains were shut off and the gardens abandoned. The people attempted to adapt to their new reality but without their life-sustaining lake, the deterioration was inexorable and soon the upper valley turned into a desolate place.

This is exactly what has happened to our inner cities. Once, they were like the place by the lake—vibrant and prosperous—until the suburbs came along and drained them of their capital. In a capitalist society, the garden always grows wherever the capital flows. Now those of us who inhabit the urban cores of our society are fighting for some of that diminishing capital.

We have in America a Robin Hood in reverse syndrome—we take from the poor and give to the rich.

Cities Harmed by Urban Sprawl

Urban sprawl and a systematic disinvestment from our cities underlie the seemingly endemic social problems of America. It's a peculiar phenomenon that has led to economic and racial isolation, disparities in political power, the disappearance of an urban agenda in national policy, the weakening of unions, and a massive destruction of the environment.

St. Louis and Buffalo, once cities of populations over 600,000, now have around 300,000 residents. Likewise Cleveland and Detroit, once with populations of 800,000 and 1.8 million respectively, have halved their populations. The consequent effect on city services, property values, commercial enterprises, job opportunities, schools, and congregations has been catastrophic. Only the poor are left behind.

Thirty-five years ago Gary, Indiana was a city full of promise with its prosperous steel mills and the nation's first black mayor of a major city. If you were to drive through Gary today you would think that it had been systematically fire bombed. The city has lost tens of thousands of homes and the downtown area is a boarded up ghost town with its abandoned Holiday Inn and convention center. There is not enough money to support good schools and other city services.

However, if you were to take a helicopter ride and survey the region around Gary, you would see that some 40,000 new homes, new churches, and a mall—one of the largest in the country—have sprung up in the suburbs of Gary. It is a prime example of what urban sprawl does to a metropolitan region where there is little actual population growth. For every home built in the suburbs, a home will be abandoned in the city; for every mall created, whole urban commercial districts will be devastated; for every suburban church built, a city church will wither.

The irony of this tragedy is that the city of Gary actually subsidized its own demise when it subsidized the water, sewer, and utility lines for its suburbs. Money that could have been used to fix its streets was used to build expressways and roads in the suburbs.

The Transfer of Wealth

We have in America a Robin Hood in reverse syndrome—we take from the poor and give to the rich. People in our inner cities need to go to the suburbs to shop. There is not a single Sears store in the city of Detroit and every time a city resident needs a Diehard battery, he or she is subsidizing education and services for wealthier people in the suburbs.

Minnetonka, a suburban development just outside the Twin Cities area in Minnesota, is another example of such a transfer of wealth. Of the $360 million in public monies spent on creating it, only about $30 million came from the people in the new suburb. The people in the cities and older suburbs provided the balance, which would have been better spent on repairing streets and yes, some important bridges.

Real property, which for most Americans provides a hedge against retirement or the capital to start a business or send children to college, has been stagnant or declining in value in many urban areas. John A. Powell, founder and president of Ohio State University's Kirwan Institute, says that economic well being should be measured not by income but by equity. He tells the sad story of his father and his friend, both war veterans who obtained Veteran Administration (VA) loans to buy homes.

Owing to a law restricting the use of VA loan monies to integrate communities, John Powell Sr., an African American, could not buy a home in the newly created suburbs, while his white friend could not buy in the Detroit inner city. Both homes cost the same, but 30 years later, the white veteran's suburban home was worth over $350,000, whereas the black veteran's home was still worth only $15,000. The situation is tantamount to stealing over $300,000 from an African American family. Multiply this by 10 million and you get some idea of how institutional racism plays itself out in the United States.

Urban sprawl, because it concentrates poverty, puts tens of thousands of America's children on the economic conveyor belt to the junk heap of history.

The Peculiar Phenomenon of Urban Sprawl

Professor Powell makes the startling statement that the net capital worth of the entire black community in America is zero. As much is owed as is owned. But the net worth of the white community is $9.0 trillion. This disparity is largely a result of the creation of urban sprawl.

Currently, congressional districts from the suburbs outnumber urban and rural districts combined. So, the majority of those who make our laws in congress are uninterested in the issues facing city dwellers. And unions tend to lose their power the farther they go from the city.

Perhaps the most tragic victims of this peculiar phenomenon are the children in our cities. The most predictive factor of success for schools is the economic status of the population they serve—the greater the concentration of poverty, the more likely that the children will do poorly. Poor children living in a middle income neighborhood will have a much greater chance of success than children living in areas of concentrated poverty where they have few role models, live in crime infested communities, and have no opportunities for summer and after school jobs. Urban sprawl, because it concentrates poverty, puts tens of thousands of America's children on the economic conveyor belt to the junk heap of history.

Urban sprawl also destroys green space. The building of houses on natural flood basins and the ever growing network of expressways with their polluting traffic pose the number one threat to the environment.

But it does not have to be this way.

Portland's Solution to Urban Sprawl

In Portland, Oregon they have created an urban growth boundary around the already developed metropolitan region. Thirty years ago, the metropolitan planning council created a policy that no government funds would be expended outside this boundary. As a result, property within the boundary is now worth a million dollars per acre; whereas, outside the boundary an acre fetches about $1,000. People can build outside the boundary but they will not have a road, sewer system, or water main built to their house. And in the event of a house fire, there is no guarantee that a fire truck will be made available, causing home insurance rates to go up.

Julius Caesar is quoted as saying: "The margin of profit for most enterprises is government subsidy." An observation that is as true today as it was 2,000 years ago. By restricting subsidies outside the metropolitan area Portland created a level playing field for African Americans. Now property values in Portland's traditional black community have increased by 10 billion dollars.

Organizing for the Sprawl

The type of issues at the heart of the urban problem are: how taxes are raised and spent, the allocation of federal and state transportation dollars, school funding formulas, land use policy, water rights, and opportunity housing. We need to stop subsidizing urban sprawl and the concentration of poverty and create a tax policy that spreads the wealth equitably across a region. We also need to mandate mixed income housing in every suburb. But the traditional model of organizing neighborhoods in urban areas to solve problems is no longer relevant because decisions affecting the urban core are not made by city hall—they are made at a regional level and governed by state law.

Those who make policy realize that the population in the urban core is now a small minority. Milwaukee, Cleveland, Detroit, Gary, Buffalo, Atlanta, St. Louis, and Oakland do not have that much clout in state politics. These cities are a minority even in their metropolitan region. To move political power we must build a much broader base and organize at the metropolitan and state wide levels.

In his book, *Who Rules America: Power Politics and Social Change*, William Domhoff asserts that the forces of sprawl combine into a cabal that wields enormous power at the state and local levels and real change can occur only when all progressive forces align.

Unions, civil rights organizations, progressive politicians, transportation activists, environmentalists, and urban neighborhoods are all negatively impacted by sprawl. And increasingly, the first and second rings of suburbs are also being affected, giving many suburban politicians an interest in curbing this ever expanding circle of destruction.

It is time for community organizing to recognize that its targeted base should expand beyond the minority and working class white communities in cities to include some middle-income suburbs as well. Combating urban sprawl offers an opportunity to create the type of coalition that Domhoff describes as necessary for change.

Our next president comes out of the community organizing tradition. A former director of a Gamaliel affiliate on the South Side of Chicago, Barack Obama understands the pernicious problems created by urban sprawl for the people in the cities. He has also constructed a powerful coalition of progressive forces in this country, which crosses race, class, and geographic boundaries. This is an optimum time for the new organizing model to take root by tapping into this emerging coalition with a fresh outlook on solving problems. By examining the racial implications of urban sprawl and committing ourselves to addressing them effectively we can begin to heal many of the seemingly incurable social problems confronting our country.

Urban Sprawl and Automobile Dependence Are Bad for Public Health

Simon Kuper and Pauline Harris

Simon Kuper is the sports columnist for the Financial Times *in London and Pauline Harris is a writer in Paris.*

It is called the "walking school bus". All over Rome, groups of children walk to school, following a set route and picking up other children at "bus stops" as they go, escorted by two adult "drivers". The *scuolabus a piedi* gets children exercising. It is proposed to spread to all Roman primary schools, and runs in other cities, too.

If modern humans are to get enough exercise, they will have to do it as part of daily life, because few people can be bothered to jog after work. That means cities need to become living gyms. That is quite a change, after decades of rule by cars. Moreover, in our cash-strapped age, the change will have to be made cheaply. Yet it can be done. Initiatives such as the walking bus are now sprouting everywhere, particularly in western Europe and on the US west coast. The contours of the city as a gym are becoming clear.

The Design of Cities

First of all, the city will have to be condensed. People are more likely to walk or cycle if they live in built-up areas, near shops, offices and schools, instead of in vast suburbs where cars are essential. Reid Ewing, urban planner at Rutgers University in New Jersey, found that inhabitants of compact places such as Manhattan were slimmer than residents of sprawling suburbs.

To make cities more compact, zoning laws must change, says J.H. Crawford, a founder of the "car-free" movement. He explains that in the industrial age, US cities rightly separated residential areas from heavy industry. However, that model of zoning is now outdated. Cities now feature not just suburbs but also "exurbs"—suburbs of suburbs.

"The underlying premise of US cities is that you will drive everywhere you go," Crawford says.

He wants people to live, work and shop in one neighbourhood. US cities have slowly begun to combat sprawl, but only up to a point. Nobody is about to flatten the exurbs; their inhabitants like their spacious homes. And modern life itself has lengthened journeys in many countries. Melvyn Hillsdon, an expert on exercise at the UK's Exeter University, says: "Data from our national travel surveys over the past few years tend to say that people travel further to work." Any increase in density of living will need to come from new-build areas. That is more easily achieved in fast-growing Asian cities than in the more established US or Europe.

The Need to Encourage Walking and Cycling

Still, even when buildings cannot be touched, city planners can nudge people to walk or cycle. Among the essentials are perfect parks and open spaces. Surveys show that the more time children and the elderly spend outside, the more they tend to exercise. But many parks struggle to compete with today's enticing indoor environments. Hillsdon says: "We've now got incredibly seductive homes: we've got home entertainment, they're generally well heated, we can date online, we can shop online. Yet we're only going to get physically active outside. This is the first generation that has to make a conscious decision to go outdoors." To push people outside, outdoor spaces must become as appealing as homes.

Streets must be reclaimed from cars. Copenhagen is the role model. The Danish capital is now a biking paradise, where half of inner-city residents cycle to work—but it was not always like that. "Copenhagen was a big gamble, a retrofit," says Hillsdon. Kristian Villadsen, associate at Gehl Architects in Copenhagen, explains: "Copenhagen has had very good urban planners. We now have bike lanes on every street in the city. People feel secure from cars, and from other people, so it's an invitation."

There is a flip side to encouraging cyclists and pedestrians: you need to discourage cars.

Similar strategies can work elsewhere—even in the US. Gehl Architects went to New York and found that its elderly and children did not walk much. So it widened pavements to make pedestrians feel safer. "We've made a very fast transformation over two years in New York," says Villadsen. "Last summer [2009] we helped close Times Square to traffic. We've made cycle lanes, and given more public space to the city. We extended the sidewalk by 3m on Broadway, so now they're calling it Broadway Boulevard. We do temporary projects that can be transformed into permanent projects. It's much easier to work like this than from a proposal."

The Need to Discourage Cars

There is a flip side to encouraging cyclists and pedestrians: you need to discourage cars. Jerry Morris, the pioneering epidemiologist of exercise, lamented shortly before he died last year aged 99: "You've got to confront the motorcar. Which no government has had the courage to confront." Yet it is feasible. Many people drive simply from habit and laziness. A quarter of English car journeys are shorter than one mile. If people have to pay for driving and especially for parking—that is, for renting a valuable urban space—they will drive less.

In Europe, Paris is leading the charge against driving. The city already offers a fleet of cheap rental bikes, and this year will add cheap rental cars. The hope is that some residents will give up their own underused cars to save money on parking. Moreover, for one month every summer, the city's Georges Pompidou expressway closes to cars and turns into an urban beach. Gradually, Parisians are learning to see cars as expensive liabilities.

That is the northern European trend. Hillsdon says British town planners now take it for granted that new neighbourhoods must favour walking, cycling and public transport. That is new, he notes: "Town planners had always been trained to move cars around efficiently."

Offices can help too. After all, most people spend the largest part of their day there. Workplaces can encourage exercise by installing bike racks, showers for cyclists or signs pointing to the stairs.

Addressing the Health Gap

Yet even cities that do everything right—those that encourage parks, pedestrians and bikes—run a risk. They might chiefly be helping the groups who already exercise most. Rich people and men exercise more than poor people and women.

A city as a gym is good not just for health. A walking city is a greener city.

British cyclists are overwhelmingly young men, notes Hillsdon. "That is a risk of putting a great emphasis on promoting cycling: you might inadvertently be increasing inequality in physical activity."

Cities are now trying to encourage the exercise-poor. For instance, elderly people might walk more if there are street benches where they can rest. Such measures can save lives. Health researchers at the University of Glasgow reported in 2008 that in neighbourhoods where poor people had good access to green spaces, their "health gap" with the rich narrowed.

A city as a gym is not a utopia. Copenhagen, Vienna and some Dutch cities are approaching this ideal. And a city as a gym is good not just for health. A walking city is a greener city. It is also a city that approximates the ideal of the great urbanist Jane Jacobs: a place of countless connections, where people are always running into each other in the neighbourhood.

A City for Cars

"Nobody walks in LA," sang the 1980s band Missing Persons. In a city famed for its beautiful people, not many Angelenos get enough exercise.

However, Los Angeles was not always that way. Once it had the biggest tram system ever built—the best public transit system in the US in its day. "Los Angelisation"—now a synonym for the spread of traffic-choked urban sprawl—came only later, and might yet be reversed.

For decades, trams, known as "Red Cars" and "Yellow Cars", swished through town. Steven Easlon, author of *The Los Angeles Railway Through the Years*, writes that some passengers "would ride for miles simply for fun". But it was the city's misfortune to grow in the automobile age. The trams peaked in the early 1900s. From the 1920s, Angelenos began moving to the suburbs and buying cars. Finally, the ailing Yellow Car system was bought and dismantled by a subsidiary of National City Lines, a company whose investors happened to include General Motors and other big oil and rubber industry companies. The Red Cars last ran in the 1960s.

By then, traffic jams were becoming common on LA's giant looping freeways. At first they caused confusion, but this soon gave way to anger. There were reports of frustrated grid-locked drivers shooting other drivers.

Now Inrix, a provider of traffic information, ranks LA as the US's most congested city. It is a vicious cycle. There is so much traffic that parents are afraid to let children walk to school, and so traffic grows on streets around schools. There has been a spate of accidents involving schoolchildren.

Just as policy decisions made LA a city for cars, not people, policy decisions can reverse the trend.

The Importance of Policy Decisions

The problem is not simply that nobody walks. In general, says J.H. Crawford, a founder of the "car-free" movement, "in LA, all the space is taken up by cars, so there's no room for anything else".

According to the LA county department of public health, 1.7m [million] local children do not live within walking distance of a park or other open space. On days of particularly bad pollution, children are discouraged from going out. No wonder almost a quarter of middle-school children in the county are obese.

Yet just as policy decisions made LA a city for cars, not people, policy decisions can reverse the trend.

In 2008, California passed a law to reduce urban sprawl. A test run for LA's first cicLAvia—an event in which runners, skaters and cyclists retake the streets from cars—is expected this spring [2010]. Improved metro and rail services are gaining passengers. There are even proposals to bring back the trams. One day, someone might walk in LA—particularly if the 4,600 miles of pavement in need of repair ever get fixed.

A City for People

It is a bizarre sight: a 60-something Viennese professor walks down a road, in front of cars, wearing an enormous contraption that itself vaguely resembles a car. The professor is Hermann Knoflacher, and the frame around his shoulders is a "Gehzeug", or walkmobile. His invention is the size of a car, and it makes a point: cars, parked or moving, take up antisocial amounts of a city's space.

In Vienna, Knoflacher is not considered bizarre. Rather, he is part of a city-wide movement to put people in motion. Its secret is not one initiative but a range of policies. The streets around the central St Stephen's Cathedral are car free, those around the Naschmarkt food market are to become so, and there are similar moves all over town.

Knoflacher, who is also global pedestrian representative of the United Nations, boasts that when he worked at the Vienna University of Technology, parking spaces were removed. You must frustrate drivers, he explains: "We cannot improve public transport if we do not increase congestion at the same time." Vienna's public transport was good to start with: in the 1970s and 1980s, when many cities scrapped their trams, it kept them.

The city has more than 1,000km [kilometers] of cycle paths. In 2008, a housing project opened specifically for cyclists. Bike City drew 5,000 applicants for its 99 flats. It offers cyclists everything from a repair garage to large lifts. Now private developers are planning their own versions of Bike City.

Viennese cyclists do not need masks against pollution. About half of the city's total area is green space, and the Danube river is clean enough for family swims. In some cities, women are wary of using parks, but in Vienna, says Sonja Wehsely, executive city councillor for public health and social affairs, "we try to perceive all policy fields from a woman's point of view". The parks have good lighting and visibility, and the pavements are wide enough for pushchairs.

It seems to work. Austria was one of a handful of European countries where the World Health Organisation found falling numbers of overweight and obese children between 2002 and 2006. And Vienna habitually stars in quality-of-life surveys.

Last year, Mercer, the human resources consultants, ranked it first in the world. It is a city for people rather than cars.

Urban Legends: Why Suburbs, Not Cities, Are the Answer

Joel Kotkin

Joel Kotkin is the Distinguished Presidential Fellow in Urban Futures at Chapman University and author of the book The Next Hundred Million: America in 2050.

The human world is fast becoming an urban world—and according to many, the faster that happens and the bigger the cities get, the better off we all will be. The old suburban model, with families enjoying their own space in detached houses, is increasingly behind us; we're heading toward heavier reliance on public transit, greater density, and far less personal space. Global cities, even colossal ones like Mumbai and Mexico City, represent our cosmopolitan future, we're now told; they will be nerve centers of international commerce and technological innovation just like the great metropolises of the past—only with the Internet and smart phones.

According to Columbia University's Saskia Sassen, megacities will inevitably occupy what Vladimir Lenin called the "commanding heights" of the global economy, though instead of making things they'll apparently be specializing in high-end "producer services"—advertising, law, accounting, and so forth—for worldwide clients. Other scholars, such as Harvard University's Edward Glaeser, envision universities helping to power the new "skilled city," where high wages and social amenities attract enough talent to enable even higher-cost urban meccas to compete.

The theory goes beyond established Western cities. A recent World Bank report on global megacities insists that when it comes to spurring economic growth, denser is better: "To try to spread out economic activity," the report argues, is to snuff it. Historian Peter Hall seems to be speaking for a whole generation of urbanists when he argues that we are on the cusp of a "coming golden age" of great cities.

Instead of overcrowded cities rimmed by hellish new slums, imagine a world filled with vibrant smaller cities, suburbs, and towns.

The only problem is, these predictions may not be accurate. Yes, the percentage of people living in cities is clearly growing. In 1975, Tokyo was the largest city in the world, with over 26 million residents, and there were only two other cities worldwide with more than 10 million residents. By 2025, the U.N. projects that there may be 27 cities of that size. The proportion of the world's population living in cities, which has already shot up from 14 percent in 1900 to about 50 percent in 2008, could be 70 percent by 2050. But here's what the boosters don't tell you: It's far less clear whether the extreme centralization and concentration advocated by these new urban utopians is inevitable—and it's not at all clear that it's desirable.

Not all Global Cities are created equal. We can hope the developing-world metropolises of the future will look a lot like the developed-world cities of today, just much, much larger—but that's not likely to be the case. Today's Third World megacities face basic challenges in feeding their people, getting them to and from work, and maintaining a minimum level of health. In some, like Mumbai, life expectancy is now at least seven years less than the country as a whole. And many of the world's largest advanced cities are nestled in relatively declining economies—London, Los Angeles, New York, Tokyo. All suffer growing income inequality and outward migration of middle-class families. Even in the best of circumstances, the new age of the megacity might well be an era of unparalleled human congestion and gross inequality.

Perhaps we need to consider another approach. As unfashionable as it might sound, what if we thought less about the benefits of urban density and more about the many possibilities for proliferating more human-scaled urban centers; what if healthy growth turns out to be best achieved through dispersion, not concentration? Instead of overcrowded cities rimmed by hellish new slums, imagine a world filled with vibrant smaller cities, suburbs, and towns: Which do you think is likelier to produce a higher quality of life, a cleaner environment, and a lifestyle conducive to creative thinking?

So how do we get there? First, we need to dismantle some common urban legends.

Perhaps the most damaging misconception of all is the idea that concentration by its very nature creates wealth. Many writers, led by popular theorist Richard Florida, argue that centralized urban areas provide broader cultural opportunities and better access to technology, attracting more innovative, plugged-in people (Florida's "creative class") who will in the long term produce greater economic vibrancy. The hipper the city, the mantra goes, the richer and more successful it will be—and a number of declining American industrial hubs have tried to rebrand themselves as "creative class" hot spots accordingly.

But this argument, or at least many applications of it, gets things backward. Arts and culture generally do not fuel economic growth by themselves; rather, economic growth tends to create the preconditions for their development. Ancient Athens and Rome didn't start out as undiscovered artist neighborhoods. They were metropolises built on imperial wealth—largely collected by force from their colonies—that funded a new class of patrons and consumers of the arts. Renaissance Florence and Amsterdam established themselves as trade centers first and only then began to nurture great artists from their own middle classes and the surrounding regions.

Even modern Los Angeles owes its initial ascendancy as much to agriculture and oil as to Hollywood. Today, its port and related industries employ far more people than the entertainment business does. (In any case, the men who built Hollywood were hardly cultured aesthetes by middle-class American standards; they were furriers, butchers, and petty traders, mostly from hardscrabble backgrounds in the czarist *shtetls* and back streets of America's tough ethnic ghettos.) New York, now arguably the world's cultural capital, was once dismissed as a boorish, money-obsessed town, much like the contemporary urban critique of Dallas, Houston, or Phoenix.

Culture, media, and other "creative" industries, important as they are for a city's continued prosperity, simply do not spark an economy on their own.

Sadly, cities desperate to reverse their slides have been quick to buy into the simplistic idea that by merely branding themselves "creative" they can renew their dying economies; think of Cleveland's Rock and Roll Hall of Fame, Michigan's bid to market Detroit as a "cool city," and similar efforts in the washed-up industrial towns of the British north. Being told you live in a "European Capital of Culture," as Liverpool was in 2008, means little when your city has no jobs and people are leaving by the busload.

Even legitimate cultural meccas aren't insulated from economic turmoil. Berlin—beloved by writers, artists, tourists, and romantic expatriates—has cultural institutions that would put any wannabe European Capital of Culture to shame, as well as a thriving underground art and music scene. Yet for all its bohemian spirit, Berlin is also deeply in debt and suffers from unemployment far higher than Germany's national average, with rates reaching 14 percent. A full quarter of its workers, many of them living in wretched immigrant ghettos, earn less than 900 euros a month; compare that with Frankfurt, a smaller city more known for its skyscrapers and airport terminals than for any major cultural output, but which boasts one of Germany's lowest unemployment rates and by some estimates the highest per capita income of any European city. No wonder Berlin Mayor Klaus Wowereit once described his city as "poor but sexy."

Culture, media, and other "creative" industries, important as they are for a city's continued prosperity, simply do not spark an economy on their own. It turns out to be the comparatively boring, old-fashioned industries, such as trade in goods, manufacturing, energy, and agriculture, that drive the world's fastest-rising cities. In the 1960s and 1970s, the industrial capitals of Seoul and Tokyo developed their economies far faster than Cairo and Jakarta, which never created advanced industrial bases. China's great coastal urban centers, notably Guangzhou, Shanghai, and Shenzhen, are replicating this pattern with big business in steel, textiles, garments, and electronics, and the country's vast interior is now poised to repeat it once again. Fossil fuels—not art galleries—have powered the growth of several of the world's fastest-rising urban areas, including Abu Dhabi, Houston, Moscow, and Perth.

It's only after urban centers achieve economic success that they tend to look toward the higher-end amenities the creative-classers love. When Abu Dhabi decided to import its fancy Guggenheim and Louvre satellite museums, it was already, according to *Fortune* magazine, the world's richest city. Beijing, Houston, Shanghai, and Singapore are opening or expanding schools for the arts, museums, and gallery districts. But they paid for them the old-fashioned way.

Nor is the much-vaunted "urban core" the only game in town. Innovators of all kinds seek to avoid the high property prices, overcrowding, and often harsh anti-business climates of the city center. Britain's recent strides in technology and design-led manufacturing have been concentrated not in London, but along the outer reaches of the Thames Valley and the areas around Cambridge. It's the same story in continental Europe, from the exurban Grand-Couronne outside of Paris to the "edge cities" that have sprung up around Amsterdam and Rotterdam. In India, the bulk of new tech companies cluster in campus-like developments around—but not necessarily in—Bangalore, Hyderabad, and New Delhi. And let's not forget that Silicon Valley, the granddaddy of global tech centers and still home to the world's largest concentration of high-tech workers, remains essentially a vast suburb. Apple, Google, and Intel don't seem to mind. Those relative few who choose to live in San Francisco can always take the company-provided bus.

When it comes to inequality, cities might even be the problem.

In fact, the suburbs are not as terrible as urban boosters frequently insist.

Consider the environment. We tend to associate suburbia with carbon dioxide-producing sprawl and urban areas with sustainability and green living. But though it's true that urban residents use less gas to get to work than their suburban or rural counterparts, when it comes to overall energy use the picture gets more complicated. Studies in Australia and Spain have found that when you factor in apartment common areas, second residences, consumption, and air travel, urban residents can easily use more energy than their less densely packed neighbors. Moreover, studies around the world—from Beijing and Rome to London and Vancouver—have found that packed concentrations of concrete, asphalt, steel, and glass produce what are known as "heat islands," generating 6 to 10 degrees Celsius more heat than surrounding areas and extending as far as twice a city's political boundaries.

When it comes to inequality, cities might even be the problem. In the West, the largest cities today also tend to suffer the most extreme polarization of incomes. In 1980, Manhattan ranked 17th among U.S. counties for income disparity; by 2007 it was first, with the top fifth of wage earners earning 52 times what the bottom fifth earned. In Toronto between 1970 and 2001, according to one recent study, middle-income neighborhoods shrank by half, dropping from two-thirds of the city to one-third, while poor districts more than doubled to 40 percent. By 2020, middle-class neighborhoods could fall to about 10 percent.

Cities often offer a raw deal for the working class, which ends up squeezed by a lethal combination of chronically high housing costs and chronically low opportunity in economies dominated by finance and other elite industries. Once the cost of living is factored in, more than half the children in inner London live in poverty, the highest level in Britain, according to a Greater London Authority study. More than 1 million Londoners were on public support in 2002, in a city of roughly 8 million.

The most advantaged city of the future could well turn out to be a much smaller one.

The disparities are even starker in Asia. Shenzhen and Hong Kong, for instance, have among the most skewed income distributions in the region. A relatively small number of skilled professionals and investors are doing very well, yet millions are migrating to urban slums in places like Mumbai not because they've all suddenly become "knowledge workers," but because of the changing economics of farming. And by the way, Mumbai's slums are still expanding as a proportion of the city's overall population—even as India's nationwide poverty rate has fallen from one in three Indians to one in five over the last two decades. Forty years ago, slum dwellers accounted for one in six Mumbaikars. Now they are a majority.

To their credit, talented new urbanists have had moderate success in turning smaller cities like Chattanooga and Hamburg into marginally more pleasant places to live. But grandiose theorists, with their focus on footloose elites and telecommuting technogeniuses, have no practical answers for the real problems that plague places like Mumbai, let alone Cairo, Jakarta, Manila, Nairobi, or any other 21st-century megacity: rampant crime, crushing poverty, choking pollution. It's time for a completely different approach, one that abandons the long-held assumption that scale and growth go hand in hand.

Throughout the long history of urban development, the size of a city roughly correlated with its wealth, standard of living, and political strength. The greatest and most powerful cities were almost always the largest in population: Babylon, Rome, Alexandria, Baghdad, Delhi, London, or New York.

But bigger might no longer mean better. The most advantaged city of the future could well turn out to be a much smaller one. Cities today are expanding at an unparalleled rate when it comes to size, but wealth, power, and general well-being lag behind. With the exception of Los Angeles, New York, and Tokyo, most cities of 10 million or more are relatively poor, with a low standard of living and little strategic influence. The cities that do have influence, modern infrastructure, and relatively high per capita income, by contrast, are often wealthy small cities like Abu Dhabi or hard-charging up-and-comers such as Singapore. Their efficient, agile economies can outpace lumbering megacities financially, while also maintaining a high quality of life. With almost 5 million residents, for example, Singapore isn't at the top of the list in terms of population. But its GDP [gross domestic product] is much higher than that of larger cities like Cairo, Lagos, and Manila. Singapore boasts a per capita income of almost $50,000, one of the highest in the world, roughly the same as

America's or Norway's. With one of the world's three largest ports, a zippy and safe subway system, and an impressive skyline, Singapore is easily the cleanest, most efficient big city in all of Asia. Other smaller-scaled cities like Austin, Monterrey, and Tel Aviv have enjoyed similar success.

It turns out that the rise of the megacity is by no means inevitable—and it might not even be happening. Shlomo Angel, an adjunct professor at New York University's Wagner School, has demonstrated that as the world's urban population exploded from 1960 to 2000, the percentage living in the 100 largest megacities actually declined from nearly 30 percent to closer to 25 percent. Even the widely cited 2009 World Bank report on megacities, a staunchly pro-urban document, acknowledges that as societies become wealthier, they inevitably begin to deconcentrate, with the middle classes moving to the periphery. Urban population densities have been on the decline since the 19th century, Angel notes, as people have sought out cheaper and more appealing homes beyond city limits. In fact, despite all the "back to the city" hype of the past decade, more than 80 percent of new metropolitan growth in the United States since 2000 has been in suburbs.

The goal of urban planners should not be to fulfill their own grandiose visions of megacities on a hill, but to meet the needs of the people living in them.

And that's not such a bad thing. Ultimately, dispersion—both city to suburb and megacity to small city—holds out some intriguing solutions to current urban problems. The idea took hold during the initial golden age of industrial growth—the English 19th century—when suburban "garden cities" were established around London's borders. The great early 20th-century visionary Ebenezer Howard saw this as a means to create a "new civilization" superior to the crowded, dirty, and congested cities of his day. It was an ideal that attracted a wide range of thinkers, including Friedrich Engels and H.G. Wells.

More recently, a network of smaller cities in the Netherlands has helped create a smartly distributed national economy. Amsterdam, for example, has low-density areas between its core and its corporate centers. It has kept the great Dutch city both livable and competitive. American urbanists are trying to bring the same thinking to the United States. Delore Zimmerman, of the North Dakota-based Praxis Strategy Group, has helped foster high-tech-oriented development in small towns and cities from the Red River Valley in North Dakota and Minnesota to the Wenatchee region in Washington State. The outcome has been promising: Both areas are reviving from periods of economic and demographic decline.

But the dispersion model holds out even more hope for the developing world, where an alternative to megacities is an even more urgent necessity. Ashok R. Datar, chairman of the Mumbai Environmental Social Network and a longtime advisor to the Ambani corporate group, suggests that slowing migration to urban slums represents the most practical strategy for relieving Mumbai's relentless poverty. His plan is similar to Zimmerman's: By bolstering local industries, you can stanch the flow of job seekers to major city centers, maintaining a greater balance between rural areas and cities and avoiding the severe overcrowding that plagues Mumbai right now.

Between the 19th century, when Charles Dickens described London as a "sooty spectre" that haunted and deformed its inhabitants, and the present, something has been lost from our discussion of cities: the human element. The goal of urban planners should not be to fulfill their own grandiose visions of megacities on a hill, but to meet the needs of the people living in them, particularly those people suffering from overcrowding, environmental misery, and social inequality. When it comes to exporting our notions to the rest of the globe, we must be aware of our own susceptibility to fashionable theories in urban design—because while the West may be able to live with its mistakes, the developing world doesn't enjoy that luxury.

Urban Sprawl Simply Reflects the Preferences of Americans

Randal O'Toole

Randal O'Toole is a senior fellow at the Cato Institute working on urban growth, public land, and transportation issues. He is also the author of Gridlock: Why We're Stuck in Traffic and What to Do About It.

On Thursday, March 18 [2010], John Stossel's show on the Fox Business News network will feature a discussion of how taxes and regulation have prevented urban areas like Cleveland from recovering from the decline of the industries that once supported those regions.

While the "stars" of the show were Drew Carey and *Reason* Magazine's Nick Gillespie, Stossel spent a few minutes on zoning and land-use regulation. When searching for someone to advocate such land-use regulation, they happened to ask James Kunstler, author of *The Geography of Nowhere*, a critique of suburbia.

Kunstler's response was emphatic. First, he called one of Stossel's other guests (okay, it was me) "a shill for the sprawl-builders." Then he added, "Please tell Stoessel [sic] he can kiss my ass." He was so proud of this response that he posted it on his blog.

The Cause of Sprawl

Kunstler is biased against mobility and low-density housing, but he must be a good writer because he has lots of fans. As soon as he posted his rude reply, the blogosphere lit up with arguments from progressive, conservative, and even libertarian

Randal O'Toole, "A Libertarian View of Urban Sprawl," *Cato@Liberty*, March 16, 2010, www.cato-at-liberty.org. Republished with permission of Cato Institute. Permission conveyed through Copyright Clearance Center, Inc.

writers claiming that sprawl is the result of central planning and zoning and therefore libertarians such as Stossel and Cato should support smart-growth policies aimed at containing sprawl.

Sprawl is "mandated by a vast and seemingly intractable network of government regulations, from zoning laws and building codes to street design regulations," claims conservative Austin Bramwell. As a result, "government planning makes sprawl ubiquitous."

Anarcho-libertarian Kevin Carson quotes *The Geography of Nowhere* as the authority for how planners like Robert Moses forced people to live in sprawl. "Local governments have been almost universally dominated by an unholy alliance of real estate developers and other commercial interests" that insisted on urban sprawl, says Carson.

Developers who risk their own money are going to make every effort to build things that people want because if they don't, the developers themselves will be the losers.

Progressive Matthew Yglesias describes sprawl as "centrally planned suburbia" and accuses libertarians of being hypocrites because they don't oppose zoning codes that mandate sprawl. He adds that "People sometimes cite Houston as an example of a libertarian-style 'no zoning' city, but this is mostly a myth" (citing a paper that finds that Houston "regulates land use almost as intricately as cities with zoning").

This is all balderdash and poppycock. People who believe it should get their noses out of Kunstler's biased diatribes and look at some real data and see how zoning actually worked before it was hijacked by authoritarian urban planners. It doesn't take much to show that areas without any zoning or regulation will—if developed today—end up as what planners call "sprawl." Until recently, all that zoning has done has been to affirm the kind of development that people want.

The Invention of Zoning

Contrary to Carson's claim, zoning was not invented by developers trying to impose their lifestyle preferences on unsuspecting Americans. The idea that realtors and developers could somehow force people to buy houses they didn't want is refuted by hundreds or thousands of real-estate developments that failed financially because they did not offer what people wanted. Unlike planners who write prescriptive zoning codes, developers who risk their own money are going to make every effort to build things that people want because if they don't, the developers themselves will be the losers.

Instead, zoning was invented by homeowners in existing developments who wanted to insure that their neighborhoods would maintain some degree of stability. When zoning was first applied, it was used almost exclusively in areas that were already developed. Those original zones merely reaffirmed the development that was already there. Single-family neighborhoods were zoned for single-family homes; apartments for multi-family; industrial for industry; and so forth.

City officials did not consider it their job to dictate what kind of homes or other buildings people should build and buy.

The Supreme Court's 1926 *Euclid* [*v. Amber*] decision was not over vacant land but an existing neighborhood of single-family homes. A realtor wanted the option of building an apartment building in this neighborhood. The court realized that an apartment building could attract higher rents if it were located in a stable neighborhood of single-family homes, but conversely it could reduce the value of the nearby homes. Rightly or wrongly, the court decided that the rights of homeowners to maintain their property values exceeded the right of one property owner seeking to boost the value of his property at everyone else's expense.

After the *Euclid* decision, most American cities zoned their neighborhoods. Planners criticize "Euclidian zoning" because most zones separate housing from other uses. But such separation was the prevailing standard in developments after about 1900, and zoning merely affirmed that standard because most of the land that was zoned was already developed.

Zoning and Market Demand

Most vacant land in a metropolitan area is outside of city limits under the jurisdiction of county governments, and until the 1960s and 1970s most states did not give counties the authority to zone (some still don't). As Robert Nelson pointed out in his book, *Zoning and Property Rights*, when cities or counties did zone vacant land, they generally put it in a "holding zone," meaning that it was zoned for a low density until some developer saw a market for something else. The developer would then ask the city or county to rezone for the market, and the city or county almost always complied.

People look at these low-density holding zones and charge that they force sprawl. It would be true if the zones were inflexible, but in fact the cities and counties were responsive to market demand: when a landowner or developer came forth with a proposal, the city or county generally reclassified the land into an appropriate zone. NIMBYs [not in my backyard] who expected that the low-density zones would remain forever were doomed to disappointment, and they often accused city/county commissioners of somehow being in the thrall of the developers. But the developers themselves were just reflecting market demand and city officials did not consider it their job to dictate what kind of homes or other buildings people should build and buy.

To his credit, Matthew Yglesias actually looks at some real data, namely the zoning code for Maricopa County, Arizona. But he misreads the code—or misleads his readers—when he implies that the densest zoning allowed is duplexes. In fact, chapter 7 of the code provides for multi-family housing with as many as 43 units per acre. An even bigger omission is the "planned area of development" (elsewhere called planned unit developments) zone in chapter 10, which allows for high-density, mixed-use developments. Every zoning code I have ever seen has included such a zoning option.

Whatever the code says, just reading it offers no idea of how flexible it is. If a significant chunk of vacant land is in one zone, but a developer thinks there is a market for another zone, most cities that haven't yet fallen into the smart-growth fad will cheerfully change the zone or allow a variance. Obviously, this wouldn't happen to a single vacant lot in the middle of an otherwise developed area, but would frequently happen to pieces of land that were, say, 100 acres or more. Maricopa's PAD zone, for example, allows anyone with 160 acres to build a classic New Urban (mixed-use, high-density) development.

American cities sprawl because Americans, like people all over the world, prefer to live in single-family homes and like to have a little land they can call their own.

The Impact of Regulation

As noted, Yglesias also points to land-use regulation in Houston, which supposedly enforces sprawl. It is true that Houston regulates such things as setbacks and building heights. But it does not regulate uses: you can build a 7-Eleven in the middle of single-family homes or an apartment building in an industrial district. To the extent that Houston has a separation of uses, it is because that is what people want. Convenience stores want to locate on busy streets where they are visible to lots of potential customers, so they don't often locate in the middle of neighborhoods of single-family homes. People don't want to live in industrial districts, so you don't see too many apartments in them.

If you don't believe Houston is unregulated, just step across the city line into Harris County or any of the eight counties adjacent to Harris County. Texas counties aren't allowed to zone, so there you will find virtually no regulation (other than building codes), yet you still find developments with the classic separation of uses and low-density development that planners derisively call sprawl.

And if you don't believe that, take a look at Wendell Cox's rental car tours of European (and other) cities. Few would argue that Europe has forced people to sprawl, yet Cox shows that European cities are rapidly spreading out with low-density developments that (as Peter Hall says on page 873 of his massive tome, *Cities in Civilization*) are "almost indistinguishable from [their] counterparts in California and Texas." (In a more recent article, Cox also refutes the completely undocumented claim that Americans are deserting the suburbs to move back to central cities.)

What People Want

American cities sprawl because Americans, like people all over the world, prefer to live in single-family homes and like to have a little land they can call their own for gardening, entertainment, and play areas. The automobile made it possible for almost everyone to achieve this dream, where before the auto only the upper classes could do so. As John Stossel noted back in 2006 (when Kunstler had accepted his invitation to be on his show), restrictions on sprawl will destroy "the lives of poor people" because they basically tell "low-income people who want back yards that they can't have one" (to which Kunstler supposedly replied, "you can't have everything").

So which is the appropriate libertarian view? To tell low-income people that they have to live in multi-family housing because social policy has made single-family homes artificially expensive? Or to simply eliminate zoning codes (which, contrary to Yglesias' claims, every libertarian I know advocates) and let people do what they want (including, if they want, living in high-density developments or low-density developments with deed restrictions providing the stability that zoning once offered)?

Sprawl is not the result of central planning and libertarians need not hesitate in their opposition to smart growth. The real hypocrites are the so-called progressives like Yglesias who claim to care about low-income and disadvantaged people yet support policies that will prevent most such people from ever owning single-family homes.

Urban Sprawl and Automobile Dependence Are Not Problems to Be Solved

Robert Bruegmann

Robert Bruegmann is professor emeritus of art history, architecture and urban planning at the University of Illinois at Chicago and author of the book Sprawl: A Compact History.

At least until recently, accepted wisdom has held that sprawl is recent, particularly American and that it has been caused by a rapid growth in automobile ownership and use. It is also widely believed that for economic, social, environmental and aesthetic reasons sprawl is bad and should be stopped. A good way of doing this, many observers believe, is to promote "Smart Growth." Higher density and more compact urban patterns, proponents believe, would lead to less "automobile dependence," more walking and transit use and, as a result, better access to jobs and other activities and a better environment.

A Misreading of History

There are several problems with this formula. The first is that the diagnosis relies on an erroneous reading of history. Sprawl is neither recent nor particularly American, and it was in full force long before the advent of the private automobile. If sprawl is the outward movement of people at lower densities without any over-arching planning or control, then sprawl is as old as cities. The reasons for this are not hard to find. Living at the center of most cities from the earliest times until very recently meant congestion, pollution and highly unsani-

Robert Bruegmann, "Sprawl and Accessibility," *Journal of Transport and Land Use*, vol. 1, no. 1, Summer 2008, pp. 5–11. Copyright © 2008 by Robert Bruegmann. All rights reserved. Reproduced by permission.

tary living conditions for most of the urban population. Whenever a new group of people had sufficient resources, many families were likely to try to escape the city, either by moving to the suburbs or getting a weekend or country house in the exurban belt beyond the suburban edge. This pattern was already fully visible in ancient Rome where those fortunate enough to have private transportation, meaning horses and carriages, were able to spend at least part of their time at the sea or in the cool hills east of the city.

In the modern world, the outward sprawl of London from the beginning of the industrial revolution until about 1950 was certainly as great as anything seen since World War II in the United States. This is not surprising since London was the largest and most affluent city in the Western world. With densities of over 100,000 people at the center, it was not just unpleasant. It was deadly. The rudimentary sanitation systems in the poorest quarters provided little protection against infection. Plagues swept through city centers at regular intervals killing off vast numbers of people. For this reason it is not surprising that as soon as they were able, families moved outward.

The advent of the railroad and public transportation made it possible to vastly increase the outward migration.

In the eighteenth century, for example, thousands of families departed the old medieval city of London. Many of the less affluent moved east toward the burgeoning industrial areas by the docks in eastern London. They only moved a short distance because their only means of getting around was walking, and they were obliged to live near their place of work. The more affluent Londoners tended to move west into the newly developed squares and terraces of what was then the suburban edge of London but is now the central West End.

These neighborhoods were much lower in density, quieter and more hygienic than those at the center of London. For many heads of household this meant a long-distance commute to jobs back in the center of London. This was only possible because of the efficiency of privately owned horse-drawn carriages. The same was true of those moving even further from the city center, to what were then remote agricultural towns in the countryside around London.

Virtually the entire history of modern cities is the history of newer and more efficient modes of transportation and the spreading outward of urban activity at ever lower densities. Every period of economic growth allowed a new group of people to move out. By the nineteenth century this had become a mass movement as even middle-class families could afford to live at some distance from the center. In response there appeared a rapid succession of new means of urban transportation.

The Increase in Transportation Options

The advent of the railroad and public transportation made it possible to vastly increase the outward migration. In the London area miles of sturdy brick row houses were built all around the suburban periphery from Camberwell and Clapham on the south to Islington and St. John's Woods in the north. For many of the families moving into these houses they were small miracles. Even the most modest row house gave them some measure of the kind of privacy, mobility and choice that were once only available to the wealthiest and most powerful urban dwellers. To an intellectual and artistic elite of the day, however, these new developments were cheap, ugly boxes put up by greedy developers that defaced the beautiful British countryside. Nor did this elite necessarily regard the mobility provided by public transit and the railroad as a blessing. The railroads "only encourage the common people to move about needlessly" opined the Duke of Wellington.

It is certainly true that the automobile was a major force in allowing sprawl to continue in the form it did in the twentieth century just as the railroad had been a powerful force in the nineteenth. But the experience of London over the previous centuries demonstrates that sprawl didn't require the automobile. Even Los Angeles, widely considered to be the automobile city par excellence, became the world's most dispersed large city already by 1900 well before the full impact of the automobile started to be felt. It was the railroad and the street car that allowed this to happen. And contrary to what many people assume, Los Angeles has been getting denser rather than less dense for at least the past half century during an era when most people have used the automobile as their primary means of getting around. The Los Angeles urbanized area (the Census Bureau's functional definition of "urban" that includes a central city and all of the surrounding land above 1,000 people per square mile) has increased in density from barely over 4,000 people per mile to over 7,000 people per square mile, making it the densest urban area in the United States. It is this increasing density, not sprawl, together with the fact that Los Angeles has one of the lowest provisions of freeway miles per capita in the nation, that has led to increasing traffic congestion in Los Angeles. This has happened despite the fact that Los Angeles has one of the most extensive transit systems and lowest car ownership rates in the country today.

Despite draconian governmental policies to inhibit automobile use and the expenditure of billions of dollars on public transportation, transit ridership in Europe has remained largely flat since World War II while automobile ownership and use have soared.

One of the things that all of these erroneous preconceptions about sprawl demonstrate is the complexity of urban systems and the way that in these complex systems almost every cause is also an effect and vice versa. Thus, rather than say, as many people do, that the automobile was a principal cause of sprawl in the twentieth century, it would probably be at least as accurate to say that a desire for lower density living was the reason automobile makers were able to transform themselves from a small industry turning out luxury products to an enormous industry making a product that has become a standard fixture in affluent households worldwide.

The Impact of the Automobile

It also suggests that all transportation means are profoundly ambiguous in their impact on the built environment. The railroad, surely a key factor in creating the dense industrial city of the nineteenth century, was also a key factor in its decentralization. Likewise the automobile, which clearly has aided in the dispersal of cities, can also play a role in making them denser.

Curiously, as Los Angeles has become more dense over the last 50 years, the large, old cities of the American East and Europe have continued to become less dense. No large European urban area now counts even 15,000 people per square mile and many, particularly highly affluent northern European urban areas like Hamburg or Copenhagen, are now less dense than Los Angeles. With this decline in density has come a spectacular rise in automobile ownership and use. Despite draconian governmental policies to inhibit automobile use and the expenditure of billions of dollars on public transportation, transit ridership in Europe has remained largely flat since World War II while automobile ownership and use have soared. Although many people like to observe that Europeans still drive less than Americans, in fact the upward trajectory of automobile ownership and automobile use have increased in Europe in almost exactly the same way as in the United States, simply with a time lag due to a lag in affluence. So, the pattern of American car ownership as it started to take off in the

1920s is almost identical to that of Europe since the 1960s. And, as the American market reaches saturation, European car ownership and use are now rising quite a bit faster than in the United States.

One of the most important reasons for the dramatic rise in automobile use everywhere has been the way it has vastly increased mobility for most people. Because the automobile, like the private horse-drawn carriage before it, allows individuals to travel directly from point A to point B whenever the owner wishes, travel times using the automobile are almost always much shorter than travel times using public transportation. This explains, for example, why average commuting times are so much longer in dense, urban areas with heavy transit use, for example Tokyo with over 11,000 people per square mile in its urbanized area, than they are in less dense regions, for example Los Angeles. This is true as we have already remarked, even though the road network in the Los Angeles area has not been expanded to keep up with population growth or the increase in density. Likewise in the Paris region, where commuting times by individuals who use the automobile are on average about 27 minutes, for those using public transportation the figure is 53 minutes. Is it any wonder that as urban dwellers become more affluent and value their time more highly they almost invariably shun slower and less comfortable means of transportation for faster, more comfortable ones?

This shift in transportation mode might also provide a hypothesis for why densities appear to be converging across the world. As Los Angeles and virtually all of the low-density but fast-growing regions of the American West increase in density while the higher-density older urban areas in the American East and Europe decline in density, they appear to be converging in a band between 5,000 and 15,000 people per square mile. It is possible that this represents a new early twenty-first century urban norm in which densities are high enough to support much traditional urban culture but still allow for most of the inhabitants to own and use automobiles.

It is true that many people in the United States and Europe today are dependent on their automobiles because there is no other viable means to meet all of their daily transportation needs.

The Issue of Automobile Dependency

The almost universal decline in density and rise in automobile ownership within the affluent world over the last several centuries undermines many of the key elements of "Smart Growth" orthodoxy.

Take, for example, the notion of "automobile dependency," so forcefully described by Peter Newman and Geoffrey Kenworthy in a series of books and articles. They have tried to argue that sprawl has led to higher energy costs, longer commutes and more highway congestion. These ideas have been strongly rebutted by Peter Gordon and Harry Richardson, among others, who have pointed out that the only reason commuting times remained fairly stable through much of the twentieth century despite an enormous increase of population in many American cities was precisely because these cities spread out. Because both jobs and housing decentralized, this allowed for the creation at the expanding periphery of road systems better than those that can be found in the center of most older cities.

It is true that many people in the United States and Europe today are dependent on their automobiles because there is no other viable means to meet all of their daily transportation needs. This is not surprising given that it usually requires a fairly high level of density, often estimated at 10,000 people per square mile, to support a substantial transportation system, and even then this system only works well where trip origins and destinations are tightly clustered, for example when one side of the trip is a place with a very high density of jobs, for example a downtown or an airport. The majority of urban territory in the affluent western world falls well below the 10,000 threshold and increasingly the dominant position central cities held as a center of jobs for an entire region is being eroded with the growth of regional sub-centers.

The Attempt to Reduce Automobile Use

In this context the phrase "automobile dependency" can seem as silly as "refrigerator dependency." It is possible for people to do without refrigerators but why would anyone choose to do so? Likewise with automobiles. There are obviously some people who can't or don't wish to drive, and they need to be accommodated. But trying to force the vast majority of citizens who would prefer driving to instead take buses and trains in an effort to assure adequate transit for those who don't drive appears doomed to failure. The needs of the first group are often completely different from the needs of the second.

Almost all objective indicators of the quality of urban life have improved markedly with their rapid decentralization over the last half century.

Of course, many advocates of Smart Growth believe that automobile travel is inherently bad for other, especially environmental, reasons. They argue that automobile driving causes pollution and leads to climate change. However, automobiles have increased in fuel efficiency and decreased their emissions to the point where the average automobile uses barely more energy per passenger mile traveled and emits no more greenhouse gases per passenger mile traveled than an average bus, and buses carry the vast majority of transit passengers in the country today. Although this may sound remarkable at first glance, it is important to remember that buses tend to get very low gasoline mileage and over 24 hours and 7 days a week the average number of people in a bus is low. The real problem with both the automobile and the bus is the fuel source. Solving this problem should be the focus of environmental policy, not trying to substitute one means of transportation for another.

Even if less automobile use were inherently desirable, there is a good deal of evidence to suggest that the new higher density, mixed use land patterns proposed by Smart Growth proponents would not, by themselves, result in any substantial increase in bus or rail use, reduction in automobile use or enhanced mobility. It appears that it would take enormous increases in density or vastly improved transit speed and in reliability to coax even half of new drivers out of their cars. If densities increased to the point where most people used public transportation, this would still involve a major increase in the number of automobile drivers within a given area guaranteeing that congestion would be much worse. And unless all of the public transit were grade-separated, the transit itself would add greatly to this congestion.

The Myth of the Golden Age

One of the worst aspects of the fight against sprawl has been the way its enemies have tended to focus their attention on reviving some imagined golden age of the past when cities were denser, and supposedly more socially just, environmentally sound and efficient. In fact this golden age never existed. Almost all objective indicators of the quality of urban life have improved markedly with their rapid decentralization over the last half century. Certainly there are enormous problems to be faced, but there is little indication that trying to force the city back into the mold of the nineteenth century industrial city will help.

In the realm of transportation, for example, the focus on sprawl, which has tended to pit private versus public transportation and transit versus the automobile, seems to have been counter-productive. Since the 1960s the drum roll of criticism of urban highways appears to have played a significant role in reducing the public's willingness to pay for more roads, but the poor performance of new transit systems has not brought any corresponding upsurge in willingness to pay for these either. Instead there have been attempts to shift funding priorities within existing transportation dollars and these shifts have usually been counter-productive from the standpoint of the transportation system as a whole. For example shifting funding from roads, which are used by the vast majority of Americans, into transit, which is used by a tiny minority, has done little to reverse the decline in modal share of transit, but it has led to decreased spending on roads and has been partially responsible for major increases in congestion. The focus of many transit advocates for rail over bus, meanwhile, has resulted in many cities in a transfer of funding from heavily used existing bus lines to lightly used new rail lines, resulting in a declining transportation capacity overall.

Trying to remake our very long-lived urban built environment so that it will force more people to ride in old fashioned buses and trains is a classic case of the tail wagging the dog.

The fight against sprawl and the resulting battle between advocates for roads and for transit has also made it much more difficult to move forward with new technologies and transportation modes. Never have the possibilities been brighter for new forms of transport that break out of the old categories of private versus public and automobile vs transit and that promise to provide some real gains in accessibility while simultaneously reducing unfortunate environmental byproducts.

The Anti-Sprawl Movement

Unfortunately the attacks on highways and sprawl have helped to destroy the consensus about infrastructure investment for the future that characterized much of the past century. From the streetcars and rapid transit lines of the late nineteenth century to the superhighways and airports of the mid-twentieth there was enormous confidence that with the building of infrastructure we could overcome many of the apparently intractable transportation problems of the past, and indeed that is what happened as the new forms of transportation enlarged enormously the range of choices available to the average American family. Particularly since the 1960s, however, there has been a change of mood which corresponds pretty closely with the growth of anti-sprawl sentiment.

A great deal of what is written about transportation today suggests either that there is no solution to urban transportation problems or that we need to push cities back into the forms they had at some previous date in history. Anti-sprawl activists were very successful with concepts like "induced demand" and slogans like "We can't build our way out of congestion" despite the obvious fact that most of the automobiles seen on newly opened highways were there because of latent demand, not newly induced demand, and many urban areas have indeed gone a long way toward building themselves out of congestion whereas those areas that have lagged behind in road building have seen congestion rise very dramatically.

It is quite likely that within the next few decades technology will shape a fundamentally new transportation picture. Using new fuel sources, smaller, more flexible vehicles on guideways or in the air, and intelligent transportation systems that can operate faster, more safely and at much higher capacity than todays systems, the implications for the city are profound. Of course we can only guess what the new transportation systems will look like. In the meantime trying to remake our very long-lived urban built environment so that it will force more people to ride in old fashioned buses and trains is a classic case of the tail wagging the dog. It is a short-term fix that will not only not solve current problems but could easily inhibit much better means of transport in the future.

CHAPTER 2

Does Urban Sprawl
Harm the Environment?

Chapter Preface

According to a 2009 report by the US Department of Agriculture Natural Resources Conservation Service, in the twenty-five-year period between 1982 and 2007 the United States converted more than forty million acres (over 62,000 square miles) of rural land to developed land. More than seventeen million acres of forest, eleven million acres of cropland, and twelve million acres of rangeland, pastures, and wetlands were converted to housing, roads, stores, airports, and other urban and suburban uses.

Some view this development of rural land as an environmental problem and many blame sprawl. Kaid Benfield, director of the Sustainable Communities and Smart Growth program at the Natural Resources Defense Council, writes, "Nothing has been worse for our environment than sprawl."[1] Critics of urban sprawl claim that the large single-family lots, long distances between residential and commercial areas, and dependence on the car that characterize the suburbs are responsible for the shrinking countryside and increased pollution. Witold Rybczynski defends that idea that denser environments are better than the suburbs for the environment: "Urban buildings, whether apartments or row houses, are more compact and energy efficient; amenities are concentrated, which encourages walking; and public transit becomes an option."[2]

However, not all see the conversion of rural land to development through urban sprawl to be a problem. Development and transportation consultant Wendell Cox claims, "Sprawl is

1. Kaid Benfield, "The Environmental Paradox of Smart Growth," *Switchboard*, April 9, 2010. http://switchboard.nrdc.org/blogs/kbenfield/the_environmental_paradox_of_d.html.

2. Witold Rybczynski, "Dense, Denser, Densest: Americans Like Their Cities Spacious. Will Concerns About Costs and the Environment Push Them to Rein in Sprawl?" *Wilson Quarterly*, Spring 2011.

caused by population growth and affluence. But the United States is a rich nation, barely 5 percent developed, with plenty of room to grow."[3] Even with the development conversion of rural land in recent decades, America still maintains over four hundred million acres of forests, more than four hundred million acres of rangeland, and over three hundred and fifty million acres of cropland, according to the Natural Resources Conservation Service. As for environmental impact, not all agree that sprawl is a problem for the environment. Regarding housing in the suburbs, Joel Kotkin asserts, "Recent studies out of Australia show that townhouses, small condos, and even single-family homes generate far less heat per capita than the supposedly environmentally superior residential towers."[4] Randal O'Toole claims that the worry about sprawl's effect on the environment is without justification: "The suburbs are no threat to America's vast farms, forests, and open spaces, and thanks to pollution controls the environmental impacts of cars are rapidly falling."[5]

There is widespread disagreement about the impact of urban sprawl on the environment. Controversy abounds over whether development in the metropolitan fringes has resulted in a crisis of lost farmland or whether skyscrapers are preferable to subdivisions. Authors in this chapter debate these and other issues related to the environmental impact of urban sprawl.

3. Wendell Cox, "The Anti-Sprawl Movement: Anti-Minority and Anti-Immigrant?" Heartland Institute, August 21, 2003. http://heartland.org/press-releases/2003/08/21/anti-sprawl-movement-anti-minority-and-anti-immigrant?artId=12738.

4. Joel Kotkin, "The War Against Suburbia," *American*, January 21, 2010. http://american.com/archive/2010/january/the-war-against-suburbia.

5. Randall O'Toole, "The War on the Working Class," *Oregon Catalyst*, March 26, 2012. http://oregoncatalyst.com/15877-war-working-class.html.

Urban Sprawl Needs to Stop in Order to Preserve Nature

Kaid Benfield

Kaid Benfield is director of the Sustainable Communities, Energy, and Transportation Program at the Natural Resources Defense Council.

For a long time, America's environmental community celebrated wilderness and the rural landscape while disdaining cities and towns. [Naturalists Henry David] Thoreau's Walden Pond and John Muir's Yosemite Valley were seen as the ideal, while cities were seen as sources of dirt and pollution, something to get away from. If environmentalists were involved with cities at all, it was likely to be in efforts to oppose development, with the effect of making our built environment more spread out, and less urban.

The Environmental Solution

We've come a long way since then, if still not far enough. We were and remain right to uphold nature, wildlife and the rural landscape as places critical to celebrate and preserve. But what we realize now, many of us anyway, is that cities and towns— the communities where for millennia people have aggregated in search of more efficient commerce and sharing of resources and social networks—are really the environmental solution, not the problem: the best way to save wilderness is through strong, compact, beautiful communities that are more, not less, urban and do not encroach on places of significant natural value. As my friend who works long and hard for a wildlife advocacy organization puts it, to save wildlife habitat we need people to stay in "people habitat."

For our cities and towns to function as successful people habitat, they must be communities where people *want* to live, work and play. We must make them great, but always within a decidedly urban, nonsprawling form. As it turns out, compact living—in communities of streets, homes, shops, workplaces, schools and the like assembled at a walkable scale—not only helps to save the landscape; it also reduces pollution and consumption of resources. We don't drive as far or as often; we share infrastructure. While recent authors such as Edward Glaeser and David Owen are sometimes excessive in extolling the virtues of urban density without giving attention to the other things that make cities attractive and successful, they are absolutely right that city living reduces energy consumption, carbon emissions and other environmental impacts.

A lot of my professional friends are committed urbanists as well as committed environmentalists. We understand the environmental advantages of urban living so thoroughly that we take it for granted that other people do, too. But we make that mistake at our—and the planet's—peril. The increased development and maintenance of strong, sustainable cities and towns will not happen without a concerted effort.

Anticipated Population Growth

A lot is riding on the outcome: 83 percent of America's population—some 259 million people—live in cities and their surrounding metropolitan areas. Somewhat astoundingly (and as I have written previously), 37 of the world's 100 largest economies are US metros. New York, for example, ranks 13th, with a $1.8 trillion economy equivalent to that of Switzerland and the Netherlands combined; Los Angeles (18th) has an economy that is bigger than Turkey's; Chicago's (21st) is larger than Switzerland's, Poland's or Belgium's.

With so much population and economic activity, it can be no wonder that our working and living patterns in cities and suburbs have enormous environmental consequences, both for community residents and for the planet. And the implications are going to intensify: over the next 25 years, America's population will increase by 70 million people and 50 million households, the equivalent of adding France or Germany to the US. With a combination of building new homes, workplaces, shops and schools and replacing those that will reach the end of their functional lives, fully half the built environment that we will have on the ground in 25 years does not now exist.

We need our inner cities and traditional communities to absorb as much of our anticipated growth as possible, to keep the impacts per increment of growth as low as possible.

These circumstances provide not just a formidable challenge but also a tremendous opportunity to get things right. Unfortunately, past practices have done a lot of damage, particularly in the latter half of the 20th century, when America severely disinvested our inner cities and traditional towns while population, investment and tax base fled for (quite literally) greener pastures. The result, as we now know all too well, has been desecration of the natural and rural landscape while leaving behind decaying infrastructure, polluted air and waterways, and distressed populations.

Bringing Cities Back to Life

Older cities and towns with shrinking revenues did what they could, but critical issues such as waste, public transportation, street and sidewalk maintenance, parks, libraries, and neighborhood schools—issues where attention and investment could have made a difference—were back-burnered or neglected altogether. Meanwhile, sprawl caused driving rates to grow three times faster than population, sending carbon and other emissions through the roof while requiring still more costly new infrastructure that was built while we neglected the old.

We cannot allow the future to mimic the recent past. We need our inner cities and traditional communities to absorb as much of our anticipated growth as possible, to keep the impacts per increment of growth as low as possible. And, to do that, we need cities to be brought back to life, with great neighborhoods and complete streets, with walkability and well-functioning public transit, with clean parks and rivers, with air that is safe to breathe and water that is safe to drink.

This, I believe, leads to some imperatives: where cities have been disinvested, we must rebuild them; where populations have been neglected, we must provide them with opportunity; where suburbs have been allowed to sprawl nonsensically, we must retrofit them and make them better. These are not just economic and social matters: these are environmental issues, every bit as deserving of the environmental community's attention as the preservation of nature.

Urban Density Is Better for the Environment than Sprawl

David Owen, interviewed by Jared Green

David Owen is a staff writer for the New Yorker *and author. Jared Green is web content and strategy manager at the American Society of Landscape Architects (ASLA) and editor of* The Dirt *blog.*

Jared Green: *In your new book,* Green Metropolis: Why Living Smaller, Living Closer, and Driving Less Are the Keys to Sustainability, *you argue that New York City is one of the most sustainable cities in the U.S. because of its high population density. While NYC is one of the world's largest cities, per capita fuel usage is low—people walk, bike, or use public transportation instead of relying on cars. Also, per capita energy usage is also low—stacked and compact apartments and businesses are more energy efficient than the national average. The environmental lessons of New York City are: live smaller, live closer and drive less. Why is this agenda central to achieving a more sustainable future?*

The Environmental Impact of Density

David Owen: New York City has the smallest per-capita carbon footprint of any American community—just 7.1 metric tons of greenhouse gases per resident per year, compared with a national average of 24.5. (Manhattan's is even smaller, and is about the same as Sweden's.) The reason is population density. Shrinking the distance between people—and, especially, between people and their destinations—reduces energy use, carbon emission, and waste in all categories. The most important factor is automobile use. Cars are bad for the environment not only because they directly consume fuel and emit pollutants, but because they facilitate the creation of far greater sources of energy profligacy and environmental damage, in form of sprawling communities, oversized dwellings, inefficient commerce, and huge networks of redundant civic infrastructure. New York City has the lowest automobile-to-resident ratio of anyplace in the United States. Fifty-four percent of the city's households, and seventy-seven percent of Manhattan's households, don't own even one car—an unimaginable deprivation almost anywhere else in the country, where there are now more registered automobiles than there are licensed drivers. And New York City households that do own cars own fewer of them and use them far less. The New York metropolitan area accounts for almost a third of all the public-transit passenger miles in the United States, and it's one of the last places in the United States where walking can be considered a primary form of transportation. Density is the reason.

In a dense city the truly important environmental issues are less likely to be things like solar panels on building roofs than they are to be old-fashioned quality-of-life concerns.

New York City looks so different from so much of the rest of the country that its environmental examples aren't easy to apply—and even New Yorkers tend not to appreciate their power. (No one is more surprised than a Manhattanite to be told that Manhattanites are the nation's lowest per-capita energy consumers.) But dense urban centers offer one of the few plausible templates for addressing some of the world's most discouraging environmental ills, including climate change. We need to find ways to reduce the size of our living spaces, and decrease the distance between ourselves and our destinations, and begin to wean ourselves away from our near total dependence on automobiles. I spoke with one energy expert, who, when I asked him to explain why per-capita energy consumption was so much lower in Europe than in the United States, said, "It's not a secret, and it's not the result of some miraculous technological breakthrough. It's because Europeans are more likely to live in dense cities and less likely to own cars." In European cities, as in Manhattan, in other words, the most important efficiencies are built-in. And for the same reasons.

Environmental Investments for Cities

You argue that the best environmental investment a city can make should focus on how to make a city more attractive and tolerable for people to live closer together. For example, while planting trees in a neighborhood is important for improving air quality, trees are more important for creating attractive, dense neighborhoods people want to live in. Keeping crime low in a neighborhood is one of the best ways to make a dense neighborhood appealing (and therefore has a huge sustainability impact). How can cities fighting sprawl then best invest in density?

Because urban density has such high environmental value, we must find ways to shift new residential and commercial development away from places where population growth and economic growth exacerbate critical environmental problems and toward places where population growth and economic growth help to relieve them. For American cities, that will mean first understanding and then extending the benefits of population density and the thoughtful mixing of uses, as well as acknowledging that in a dense city the truly important environmental issues are less likely to be things like solar panels on building roofs than they are to be old-fashioned quality-of-life concerns like education, culture, crime, street noise, bad smells, resources for the elderly, and the availability of recreational facilities—all of which affect the willingness of people to live in efficient urban cores rather than packing up their children and fleeing to the suburbs.

Issues like these can be tough for traditional environmentalists to come to terms with, because they don't feel green: Where are the organic gardens and the backyard compost heaps? Planting trees along city streets, always a popular initiative, has high environmental utility, but not for the reasons that people usually assume: trees are ecologically important in dense urban areas not because they provide temporary repositories for atmospheric carbon—the usual argument for planting more of them—but because their presence along sidewalks makes city dwellers more cheerful about dwelling in cities. Unfortunately, much conventional environmental activism has the opposite effect, since it reinforces the view that urban life is artificial and depraved, and makes city residents feel guilty about living where and how they do.

Discouraging Automobile Use

Some argue that city living can add years to your life. You cite research by Eleanor Simonsick at the National Institute on Aging, who pointed out that "New York is literally designed to force people to walk, to climb stairs—and to do it quickly." Another study concluded that every minute spent walking extends life expectancy by three minutes. The U.S. government, with its new Livable Community Partnership, and design organizations are now focused on designing healthy communities that force people to get out of their cars and walk or bike. What do you see as the most effective design tactic for creating healthy communities in places that won't resemble NYC any time soon?

City dwellers who fantasize about living in the country usually picture themselves hiking, kayaking, gathering eggs from their own chickens, and engaging in other robust outdoor activities, but what you actually do when you move out of the city is move into a car—and move your children into car seats—because public transit is nonexistent and most daily destinations are too widely separated to make walking or bicy-cling plausible as forms of transportation. Just about the first thing my wife and I did when we moved out of the city, twenty-five years ago, was gain ten pounds apiece, because we had gone from a place where we got around mainly by walk-ing to a place where nearly everything we do away from our house requires a car trip.

To get people out of their cars, you have to do two things. First, you have to create enough density to make transit, walk-ing, and bicycling conceivable, and, second, you have to make driving sufficiently expensive, inconvenient, and unpleasant to force people to consider alternatives. As Portland and Seattle have discovered, you don't get people out of their cars just by building attractive transit systems. Washington D.C. has a beautiful subway system, but no one with a car feels com-pelled to take the train because there's always a place to park.

> Most American places are arranged around the conve-nience of drivers, rather than of pedestrians.

Anyone who has spent any time in Manhattan has had the experience of being stuck in traffic in a taxicab and watching a little old lady on the sidewalk overtake them and disappear into the distance. That's a very green experience. Traffic jams are underappreciated by mainstream environmentalists.

The Shared-Space Concept

At the street level, you point to design professionals that are implementing "traffic calming" measures that make communities more pedestrian-friendly (and therefore encourage density). Some tactics include planting trees near curbs (to reduce optical width of roads), adding bike lanes and wider sidewalks, clearly marked crosswalks, speedbumps, angle parking, etc. In Europe, you point to the idea of "shared spaces" which increase the am-biguity of urban road spaces and, instead of creating more acci-

dents, actually force drivers to slow down. Please describe this "shared space" concept, a few communities that are applying this idea, and what the impact has been on car and pedestrial access.

Shared space is a technique for controlling traffic by blurring, rather than sharply delineating, the boundaries between driving areas and walking areas; by making strategic use of traffic-impeding "street furniture", such as plantings, benches, and bicycle racks; and by eliminating traffic lights, stop signs, lane markings, and other traditional controls. This sounds to many people like a formula for disaster, but the clear experience in the (mainly) European cities that have tried it has been that increasing the ambiguity of urban road spaces actually lowers car speeds, reduces accident rates, and improves the lives of pedestrians: drivers proceed more warily when they aren't completely certain what's going on. (Shared space is also actually an ancient idea, since it's pretty much the way all large public areas functioned before the rise of automobiles.)

Most American places are arranged around the convenience of drivers, rather than of pedestrians. "Right turn on red" is an anti-pedestrian concept—and one of the relatively few places in the United States where it's illegal is New York City. Anti-jaywalking laws make things easier for drivers, not for walkers.

Wild landscapes are less often destroyed by people who despise wild landscapes than by people who love them, or think they do.

The Anti-City Ethos

You quote one environmentalist who says "sprawl is created by people escaping sprawl." Henry David Thoreau in his cabin, an iconic image of man at one with nature and living self-sufficiently off the land, you argue, set the "American pattern" for a kind of "creeping residential development." Do you think many environmentalists still laud Thoreau and his like and are anti-urban?

Americans tend to think of dense cities as despoilers of the natural landscape, but urban density actually helps to preserve it. If you spread all 8.2 million New York City residents across the countryside at the population density of Vermont, you would need a space equal to the land area of the six New England states plus New Jersey, Delaware, Maryland, and Virginia—and then, of course, you'd have to find places to put all the people you were displacing. In a paradoxical way, the Sierra Club has been a contributor to residential sprawl, because its anti-city ethos, which has been indivisible from its mission since the time of John Muir, has fueled the yearning for fresh air and elbow room which drives not only the preservation of wilderness areas but also the construction of disconnected subdivisions and daily hundred-mile car commutes. Preaching the sanctity of open spaces helps to propel development into those very spaces, and the process is self-reinforcing.

Walking-as-transportation requires closely paced, accessible destinations, not broad expanses of leafy scenery.

Thoreau wasn't actually much of an outdoorsman, and his cabin was closer to the center of Concord than to any true wilderness, but for many Americans he remains the archetype—the natural philosopher guiltlessly living off the grid, a mile from his nearest neighbor. Yet he actually set a very bad example, because anyone seeking to replicate his experience needed to move another mile farther along. Wild landscapes are less often destroyed by people who despise wild landscapes than by people who love them, or think they do—by people who move to be near them, and then, when others follow, move again. From an environmental point of view, dense cities are scalable; Thoreau's cabin is not.

The Problem with Residential Yards

In the burbs (the antithesis of the dense, sustainable NYC), homeowners are spending more than $40 billion per year on 32 million acres of lawns. However, despite all this investment in residential outdoor spaces, they aren't being used. Studies cited in your book say familes only spent "negligble" amounts of time in their yards, mostly doing chores. People are admiring their yards from indoors. Additionally, only six percent of children now regularly play outside on their own. It seems people are getting some psychological benefit from viewing their yards but how do you think residential landscapes should be re-developed so people re-engage with nature? Some argue for returning yards to nature, recreating larger ecosystems through tiny patches across residential areas.

In terms of environmental impact, what grows in a yard is probably less important than the yard's size. Yards stretch the distance between people and their destinations and therefore reinforce our dependence on automobiles. The problem with almost any initiative aimed at "re-engaging people with nature" is that it tends to encourage the very kind of sprawling, wasteful residential development that threatens unspoiled areas in the first place. The way to protect natural landscapes is to concentrate human development, not to spread it out so that each of us can claim a small piece of it as our very own.

Environmentalists and urban planners sometimes say that, in order to get people out of their cars and onto their feet, developed areas need become more like the country, by incorporating extended "greenways" and other attractive, vegetated pedestrian corridors. It's true that such features, along with parks and natural areas, can encourage some people to take walks. But, if the goal is to get people to embrace walking as a form of practical transportation, oversized greenways can actually be counterproductive. Walking-as-transportation requires closely paced, accessible destinations, not broad expanses of leafy scenery. If you want to see people moving around under their own power under the sky, don't go to the country or the suburbs; go downtown.

The Impact of Green Construction

Finally, you are fairly critical of LEED [Leadership in Energy and Environmental Design], saying there are too many LEED platinum buildings in the middle of nowhere that people then need to drive to—this is the result of "LEED brain," a myopic focus on prerequisities and credits. How would you like to see LEED, LEED-Neighborhood Development (ND), Sustainable Sites Initiative, and other important rating systems, evolve? Do they need to incorporate population density differently?

LEED has been beneficial in some ways. It has raised awareness of the environmental implications of building in general, and has helped to spread public awareness and acceptance of various green construction practices. It has also prompted the upgrading of building codes in some parts of the country, has increased awareness of the possibility of recycling many kinds of demolition and construction waste, and has helped to raise manufacturing standards for building components. But LEED is expensive and cumbersome to implement, and it has encouraged the widespread public perception that emission-reduction and energy efficiency are premium add-ons, achievable only with high-priced technology and large teams of advisers, and therefore beyond the reach of ordinary people. LEED is also mainly concerned with individual building features, and has historically given little recognition to how buildings truly function in the communities of which they are a part—or how they function over time, after the awards have been handed out. The cachet and marketing power that come with a LEED designation have encouraged developers to pile on high-visibility, low-return features—such as non-functioning photovoltaic panels, economically unjustifiable fuel cells, and expensive computer-controlled lawn-watering systems—while ignoring simpler, lower-cost measures that are either less conspicuous or less rewarded by LEED.

A critical article about LEED in *Fast Company* in 2007 quoted David White, a climate engineer, who said, "Unfortunately, the exuberant creative stuff—the expensive buzz words such as 'geothermal,' 'photovoltaic,' 'double façade,' and 'absorption chiller'—only makes sense when the basic requirements, such as a well-insulated, airtight façade with good solar control are satisfied." LEED has evolved in some ways, but White's criticism still applies. LEED is also far too building-centric, despite initiatives like LEED-ND. The Green Building Council just awarded my state's first residential platinum designation, for a new house that has every conceivable eco-gizmo but is situated more than six miles from the nearest supermarket, on 13 acres of former farmland. The draftiest apartment in Manhattan is greener than that.

Opposition to Infill Development Promotes Sprawl and Harms the Environment

Josh Harkinson

Josh Harkinson writes about the economy, the national Occupy movement, and a wide range of political issues in Mother Jones *magazine.*

Editor's Note: In August 2010 the Alameda City Council voted to terminate the agreement with SunCal and halt its proposal for development of Alameda Naval Air Station.

One of the hottest pieces of real estate in the San Francisco Bay Area is a 1,500-acre expanse of concrete, landfill, and asbestos-stuffed warehouses. Shuttered since 1997, the Alameda Naval Air Station occupies one-third of Alameda, an island next door to downtown Oakland known as a time warp to 1950s architecture and Kiwanis Club folksiness. For nearly a decade, the well-heeled enclave has had its eyes on the old air base, now dubbed Alameda Point. And why not? It's smack on the eastern edge of the bay, with spectacular views of the San Francisco skyline, and just minutes from the cities to which suburbanites commute for an hour or more. It's a developer's dream—all the more so because building there would displace little more than a gigantic monthly flea market.

A Development Proposal

In 2007, developers announced a billion-dollar-plus plan to rebuild Alameda Point. SunCal Companies envisioned a complex featuring 1,000 detached single-family homes, 2,000

Josh Harkinson, "Yes in My Backyard: Memo to Urban Environmentalists: Don't Fight Development—Embrace It," *Mother Jones*, vol. 35, no. 3, May/June 2010, pp. 55–57.

townhomes, and 1,000 condos in three-story buildings built with the latest in energy-efficient design: passive solar, geo-thermal heat pumps, and gray-water systems. Historic buildings would be preserved, and 25 percent of the units would be set aside as affordable housing. There would be 150 acres of parks, miles of trails, shops, and offices, and dedicated ferry and bus lines to Oakland and San Francisco. The local chapter of the Greenbelt Alliance endorsed it, calling it "the epitome of smart growth."

Promoting infill development . . . instead of building more subdivisions could effectively conserve the amount of energy produced by 2,800 power plants and could prevent some 26 trillion miles of driving.

Yet despite its green bona fides—and the promise of adding desperately needed affordable housing in the heart of the Bay Area—environmental activists, the local historic preservation society, and even Alameda's mayor came out against the plan. They argued that the deal gave the developer too much power, could release toxic chemicals, and would "change the character of Alameda." Driving his BMW past the naval base's peeling hangars, David Howard, a 41-year-old Internet marketer and the head of Save Our City! Alameda, stressed that he's "not anti-everything about high density." But he felt that the Alameda Point project didn't go far enough environmentally. Instead, he envisioned transforming the base into a "green technolopolis" that would invent a silver-bullet solution to the climate crisis. His plan didn't include any housing, but there'd be a wind farm, a solar power plant, a factory for the electric carmaker Tesla Motors, and an "ecobranch" of the cash-strapped University of California. "It's a wonderful location," he concluded. "It's a problem that needs to be solved. Why not do it here, in Alameda?"

The Alameda Point project also brushed up against a nearly 40-year-old density ban, which the *Oakland Tribune* has called "the 'third rail' of Alameda politics." The popular measure, which effectively caps growth on the island, has helped preserve the city's small-town feel; its population has hovered around 75,000 for decades. To get built, Alameda Point would need an exemption. When the matter was put before Alameda voters this February [2010], an overwhelming 85 percent rejected it.

The Opposition to Infill Development

More than just another triumph of NIMBYism [not-in-my-backyardism], the failure of Alameda Point is also a lesson in how fighting local growth can undermine the larger environmental values that many NIMBYs believe in. By 2050, the United States can expect to add as many as 200 million people. Demographers predict that they'll require 90 million houses and 140 billion square feet of office and other nonresidential space—the equivalent of replacing all the country's existing buildings. If we keep building in the way we do now, suburbs will gobble up a New Mexico–size amount of open space in the next 40 years. More suburbs mean more freeways and more cars, which means that by mid-century, Americans will clock 7 trillion miles per year—twice as much mileage as we do now. The alternative to this metastasizing, car-dependent sprawl is population density. And that means squeezing more people into cities and inner suburbs like Alameda. According to the Greenbelt Alliance, the Bay Area could absorb another 2 million residents by 2035 without expanding its physical footprint.

Cities are also essential to stemming climate change. As Kaid Benfield, director of the Natural Resources Defense Council's [NRDC's] Smart Growth program explains, "The city is inherently energy efficient. Even the greenest household in an outlying location can't match an ordinary household downtown." Heating an apartment uses as much as 20 percent less energy than heating a single-family home of the same size. Promoting infill development—the practice of filling empty urban space or replacing older buildings with bigger ones—instead of building more subdivisions could effectively conserve the amount of energy produced by 2,800 power plants and could prevent some 26 trillion miles of driving. All told, if the United States focuses on increasing urban density, our greenhouse gas emissions in 2050 could be as much as 20 percent lower than they'd be in the sprawl scenario.

Yet infill development is often rejected by environmental and sustainability advocates. The chief opponent of a proposal to build taller buildings in downtown Berkeley also heads a group that urges cities "to take real action to address the causes of global warming." The San Francisco Board of Supervisors' hyperliberal wing recently proposed banning new high rises downtown—never mind that these mixed-use buildings would help finance a new public transit hub and a park that the same supervisors support. Last year, wealthy Seattle residents allied with an affordable-housing advocate to scuttle a plan to build new housing next to a light-rail line. Such knee-jerk NIMBYism isn't limited to the West Coast: New York's Long Island Pine Barrens Society is opposing a plan to build a compact, $4 billion "mini-city" on unused hospital grounds that would preserve one-third of its 460 acres as open space.

Walking the anti-density, pro-environment line can be tricky. "Our group is not the most progressive group out there in terms of promoting infill development," concedes Kent Lewandowski, chair of the Northern Alameda County Group of the Sierra Club, which declined to support Alameda Point. "But our group does get it in terms of climate change and the impact of sprawl. It's like we want everything. There is definitely—I won't say hypocrisy—but there is a contradiction of sorts."

Environmentalists' Response to Urban Density

Environmentalists have long had an uneasy relationship with urban density. In what may be the first screed against infill development, Henry David Thoreau wrote, "Deliver me from a city built on the site of a more ancient city, whose materials are ruins, whose gardens are cemeteries. The soil is blanched and accursed there." The Sierra Club was born of a desire to escape what John Muir called "the death exhalations that brood in the broad towns in which we so fondly compact ourselves," where "we are sickly, and never come to know ourselves." That ethos fueled the "back to the land" movement, but a less-crunchy variation of it also drove the explosion of commuter suburbs that environmentalists love to hate. A postwar ad for a New York suburb invited buyers to "escape from cities too big, too polluted, too crowded, too strident to call home."

Holding infill projects to impossibly high standards is an easy way to block them.

Determined to make cities more livable, environmentalists have promoted parks and public transit, fought freeways and factories, and portrayed developers as the ultimate bad guys. But these well-intentioned efforts to curb the Robert Moses-style excesses of urban development had unintended consequences. Strict limits on building height and attempts to squeeze ever-larger concessions from urban developers (but not suburban ones) drove up the cost of housing in many cities—sending builders and home buyers looking for open space. "It's a situation that has unfairly favored sprawl," says NRDC's Benfield. SunCal developer Pat Keliher says that many of his colleagues simply avoid the cost of battling urban skeptics by building on out-of-town farmland: "It's the old adage—cows don't talk."

In the early '90s, a new movement of architects and planners known as the New Urbanism targeted sprawl by recognizing that cities should grow—but smartly and sustainably. In an effort to bridge the divide between developers and environmentalists, they replaced parking lots and tract houses with compact apartments and pedestrian-friendly streets. Yet some of the most vocal critics of sprawl have been reluctant to embrace this vision. Mike Davis, the author of *City of Quartz* and the Jeremiah of suburban Los Angeles, says, "What the New Urbanists tend to produce are projects that lack one of the pivotal elements of their whole philosophy—that there is no minority, or there is no economic heterogeneity, or there's no mass transit, or there are no jobs."

The Alternative to Development

Holding infill projects to impossibly high standards is an easy way to block them. But NIMBYs' feel-good environmental objections to development can be proxies for less politically correct fears about traffic, low-income neighbors, and falling property values, says Jeremy Madsen, executive director of the Greenbelt Alliance. In the case of Alameda Point, he adds, "That's frankly why we wanted to come out with a strong statement of support."

Still, some cities and states have begun to recognize that urban development—even when it's imperfect—is inherently better than the alternative. Since 2007, California Attorney General Jerry Brown has sued or sent warnings to 45 cities for not following a law requiring them to account for their development plans' carbon footprints. He's forced San Bernardino County to mitigate its sprawl with green building technologies and gotten the Bay Area suburb of Pleasanton to lift a cap on new housing. In 2008, California passed a landmark law that provides incentives for municipal planners to promote climate-friendly land uses such as building apartments around transit stops. A two-tier permitting system that encourages building in more densely developed areas while increasing oversight on the suburban fringe is in use in Florida, Cape Cod, and Portland, Oregon. New York City now requires its planning commission to approve or deny new buildings in less than seven months, preventing costly, protracted showdowns.

"If true environmentalists do not reject the NIMBYs that are preventing the densification and building of cities," says Andres Duany, the architect who designed Seaside, Florida, a project credited with launching the New Urbanism, "environmentalism itself is going to become questionable." Ultimately, the challenge is figuring out how to address NIMBYs' legitimate local concerns while encouraging them to see the bigger picture. "People have seen such crappy development for so many decades now that they have every right to demand that new development be as sensitive and green as possible," says Benfield. "But I do think the opposition is often misplaced."

By the time David Howard and I wrapped up our tour of the naval base, his green technolopolis pitch had given way to a sort of greatest hits of anti-development arguments: Alameda Point would increase crime and block views. It would displace the rabbits who live by the runway. It was racist, because increased traffic on the island would blow exhaust into minority neighborhoods on the mainland. Not to mention that the whole thing might be wiped out by a New Orleans-style deluge precipitated by our carbon-intensive lifestyle. The polar ice caps are melting, he explained, threatening low-lying areas like Alameda Point. "All the people in there—the low-income people—they're gonna be flooded out!"

Vanishing Farmland: How It's Destabilizing America's Food Supply

Bonnie Erbé

Bonnie Erbé is a journalist and host of the PBS program To the Contrary.

Food security. Sounds boring, eh? It's not something talked about very often, but the fact is America's rising population is creating no small amount of peril in the food-supply chain. Farmland is disappearing at an alarming rate as farms are sold off and developed into suburban housing, shopping malls and transportation systems.

The Loss of Agricultural Land

The American Farmland Trust is the only national environmental organization devoted entirely to preserving farms. On its Web site are the following statistics:

- The nation lost farm and ranch land 51 percent faster in the 1990s than in the 1980s.

- We're losing our best land—most fertile and productive—the fastest.

- Our food is increasingly in the path of development.

- Wasteful land use is the problem, not growth itself.

Julia Freedgood, managing director of Farmland and Communities, of the Farmland Trust, told me in an interview, "We're losing about a million acres a year, so over the course of the last 30 years since American Farmland Trust has been in existence, that's about 30 million acres."

There's a healthy debate evolving in environmental circles about disappearing farmland and whether the loss could become so great as to threaten our ability to feed ourselves. Some environmentalists see farmland loss as largely an East Coast phenomenon.

Caroline Niemczyk, a board member of the Trust for Public Land, told me in an interview, "In the East Coast it's really a problem. We have enormous stretches of farmland in the Midwest and the far West, and that's of all types ranching, and citrus production in California, vegetables. We've got a lot of mixed use in the Mississippi Valley, but we are finding in the East Coast that it's harder and harder to maintain what really have become small family farms."

Americans have done nothing but tear up farmland for development in ever larger chunks to feed our voracious appetite for housing first, and worry about food production later.

Other environmentalists say farmland supply in the West is also on the decline. They agree that while vacant land is still more widely available in the West, it is not prime farmland. Farms are being paved over in California more quickly than in most eastern states. In California, which used to host an abundance of prime farmland, one of every six acres developed in California since the Gold Rush was paved over between 1990 and 2004.

The Lack of Smart Growth

Most environmentalists see something called smart growth as the solution, which Freedgood describes as smarter urban planning: "What we need is to actually have better cities, more livable cities, tighter-knit communities, more compact development, make more land available for farming so that we can feed more people."

The concept of smart growth became trendy in the 1970s. In the intervening 40 years, Americans have done nothing but tear up farmland for development in ever larger chunks to feed our voracious appetite for housing first, and worry about food production later. We're gluttons for suburban sprawl. On the other hand, our political will for smart growth is nonexistent. A large percentage of what has been developed, never to be reclaimed, was built close to or on prime farmland. The reason was early American farmers needed to quickly transport fresh crops from farms to markets in more heavily populated areas. As cities grew over time, they expanded and consumed the best farmland.

This trend is exacerbating even today. In the 1990s, according to the Farmland Trust, prime land was developed 30 percent faster, proportionally, than the rate for non-prime rural land. Marginal farmland depletes a greater percentage of natural resources than prime land when it is farmed. It requires more water and irrigation to grow crops and produces a lower yield.

The Farmland Trust also reports some 86 percent of U.S. fruits and vegetables and 63 percent of dairy products are produced on prime farmland in urban-influenced areas, or near cities. That means much of that land will soon be consumed by development, too, if present trends continue. According to Freedgood, we're already short of what we need to meet America's appetite for fresh produce: "There's new data from the economic research service that shows that we're 13 million acres short of fruit and vegetable production to meet everybody's daily requirements."

The Dangers of Foreign Dependence

As the supply of prime farmland and fresh produce dwindle, Americans in turn grow more and more dependent on imported foods. According to the U.S. Department of Agriculture, we now import 79 percent of fish and shell fish, 32 percent of fruits and nuts and 13 percent of vegetables.

When we import more food, we increase our trade balance deficit, we spend much more food money on fuel for transportation, and we rely more heavily on other countries—so disruptions in those markets affect our food prices and supply chain. We are not yet at the point where we are so dependent on foreign foods we could starve if we suddenly lost access to overseas markets. But as Freedgood points out, there's one problem few people consider when the topic of imported food is raised:

"There's a high correlation between ... lack of food access and obesity, and if you're not producing enough fruits and vegetables and the price of fruits and vegetables is expensive, then those aren't the foods that people are choosing to eat. They're choosing to eat the cheap foods that tend to be really high in calories and salt and sugar and so on."

Any Volvo-driving, Brie-eating yuppie can tell you urban farmer's markets are all the rage and there seem to be more of them than in prior decades. But locally grown food still comprises a very small percentage of fresh foods sold on a national scale. So with dependence on foreign foods rising and development of prime farmland growing ever more rapidly, what else can be done to prevent over-development of farmland? The sad answer is, nothing the American populace seems to want to stomach right now.

Stopping Urban Sprawl Will Not Help the Environment

Robert Bruegmann

Robert Bruegmann is professor emeritus of art history, architecture, and urban planning at the University of Illinois at Chicago and author of Sprawl: A Compact History.

If you really want to see urban sprawl, take a look at London.

Historical Opposition to Sprawl

Yes, it's true that Britain has some of the toughest anti-sprawl measures in the world today. But I mean 19th-century London—the miles and miles of brick row houses in Camberwell and Islington. If sprawl is the outward spread of settlement at constantly lower densities without any overall plan, then London in the 19th century sprawled outward at a rate not surpassed since then by any American city.

London's sprawl was attacked just like sprawl today. Although the middle-class families moving into those row houses were thrilled to have homes of their own, members of the artistic and intellectual elite were nearly unanimous in their condemnation. They castigated the row houses as ugly little boxes put up by greedy speculators willing to ruin the beautiful countryside in order to wrest the last penny out of every square inch of land. They were confident that they would become slums within a generation. The Duke of Wellington spoke for many when he denounced the railroads that made these suburban neighborhoods possible as only encouraging "common people to move around needlessly."

Of course, today these neighborhoods are widely considered to be the very essence of central London, the kind of place that the current elite feels must be protected at all cost from the terrible development going on at the new edge of the city. And so it has gone with every major boom period in urban history, from the ancient Romans until today. As each new group has moved up to newer and better housing by moving out from the central city, there has always been another group of individuals ready to denounce the entire process.

Modern Complaints About Sprawl

Today, the complaints about sprawl are louder than ever, but as in the past, they are built on an extremely shaky foundation of class-based aesthetic assumptions and misinformation. If history is any guide, some modern anti-sprawl prescriptions will prove as ineffective as the Duke of Wellington's. Others will actually backfire.

There is no reason to assume that high-density living is necessarily more sustainable or liable to damage the environment than low-density living.

Even many of the most basic facts usually heard about sprawl are just wrong. Contrary to much accepted wisdom, sprawl in the U.S. is not accelerating. It is declining in the city and suburbs as average lot sizes are becoming smaller, and relatively few really affluent people are moving to the edge. This is especially true of the lowest-density cities of the American South and West. The Los Angeles urbanized area (the U.S. Census Bureau's functional definition of the city, which includes the city center and surrounding suburban areas) has become more than 25% denser over the last 50 years, making it the densest in the country.

This fact, together with the continued decline in densities in all large European urban areas, coupled with a spectacular rise in car ownership and use there, means that U.S. and European urban areas are in many ways converging toward a new 21st-century urban equilibrium. In short, densities will be high enough to provide urban amenities but low enough to allow widespread automobile ownership and use. The same dynamics are at work in the developing world. Although urban densities there are much higher than anything seen in the affluent West, they are plummeting even faster.

The Environmental Impact of Sprawl

A lack of reliable information underlies many of the complaints against sprawl. Take just one example that is considered by many the gravest charge of all; that sprawl fosters increased automobile use; longer commutes; and more congestion, carbon emissions and, ultimately, global warming.

There is no reason to assume that high-density living is necessarily more sustainable or liable to damage the environment than low-density living. If everyone in the affluent West were to spread out in single-family houses across the countryside at historically low densities (and there is plenty of land to do this, even in the densest European counties), it is quite possible, with wind, solar, biomass and geothermal energy, to imagine a world in which most people could simply decouple themselves from the expensive and polluting utilities that were necessary in the old high-density industrial city. Potentially, they could collect all their own energy on-site and achieve carbon neutrality.

Certainly the remedy usually proposed by the anti-sprawl lobby—increasing densities and encouraging public transit—will not solve the global warming problem. Even if all urban dwellers the world over were brought up to "ideal" urban consumption standards—say, that of a Parisian family living in a small apartment and using only public transportation—it would not reduce energy use and greenhouse emissions, since it would require such large increases in energy use by so many families who today are so poor they can't afford the benefits of carbon-based energy.

Unless we deliberately keep most of the world's urban population in poverty, packing more people into existing cities won't solve anything. The solution is finding better sources of energy and more efficient means of doing everything. As we do this, it is quite possible that the most sustainable cities will be the least dense.

The Attempt to Halt Sprawl

But let's assume for a moment that I'm entirely wrong and that sprawl is terrible. Could we stop it if we wanted to?

The record is not encouraging. The longest-running and best-known experiment was the one undertaken by Britain starting right after World War II. At that time, the British government gave unprecedented powers to planners to remake cities and took the draconian step of nationalizing all development rights to assure that these plans could be implemented. The famous 1944 Greater London plan, for example, envisioned a city bounded by a greenbelt. If there happened to be any excess population that couldn't be accommodated within the greenbelt, it was supposed to be accommodated in small, self-contained garden cities beyond the belt.

The reason [urban sprawl] has become the middle-class settlement pattern of choice is that it has given them much of the privacy, mobility and choice once enjoyed only by the wealthiest and most powerful.

Did the plan work? In one sense it did: The greenbelt is still there, and some people consider that an aesthetic triumph. But the plan certainly did not stop sprawl. As usual, the planners were not able to predict the future with any accuracy. The population grew, household size declined and affluence rose faster than predicted. Development jumped right over the greenbelt—and not into discreet garden cities, because this policy was soon abandoned.

The ultimate result was that much of southeastern England has been urbanized. Moreover, because of the greenbelt, many car trips are longer than they would have been otherwise, contributing to the worst traffic congestion in Europe.

The Concept of Sprawl

Finally, since the 1990s, with a new push to try to prevent greenfield development outside the belt, land and house prices have skyrocketed in London, creating an unprecedented crisis in housing affordability there and in virtually every other place that has tried extensive growth management.

Certainly sprawl has created some problems, just as every settlement pattern has. But the reason it has become the middle-class settlement pattern of choice is that it has given them much of the privacy, mobility and choice once enjoyed only by the wealthiest and most powerful.

Sprawl in itself is not a bad thing. What is bad is the concept of "sprawl" itself, which by lumping together all kinds of issues, some real and important and some trivial or irrelevant, has distracted us from many real and pressing urban issues. It also provides the dangerous illusion that there is a silver bullet solution to many of the discontents created by the fast and chaotic change that has always characterized city life.

Urban Sprawl Does Not Consume Too Much Agricultural Land

Wendell Cox

Wendell Cox is head of Demographia, an international public policy and consulting firm, who specializes in urban policy, transportation, and demographics.

There are few more bankrupt arguments against suburbanization than the claim that it consumes too much agricultural land. The data is so compelling that even the United States Department of Agriculture says that "our Nation's ability to produce food and fiber is not threatened" by urbanization. There is no doubt that agricultural production takes up less of the country's land than it did before. But urban "sprawl" is not the primary cause. The real reason lies in the growing productivity of American farms.

The Growth in Agricultural Productivity

Since 1950, an area the size of Texas plus Oklahoma (or an area almost as large as France plus Great Britain) has been taken out of agricultural production in the United States, *not including* any agricultural land taken by new urbanization. That is enough land to house *all* of the world's urban population at the urban density level of the United Kingdom.

Even with less land, agriculture's performance has been stunning. According to US Department of Agriculture data, US farm output rose 160% between 1950 and 2008. Productivity per acre rose 260%. In particular, California's farms—often cited as victims of sprawl—have done quite well. Between 1960 and 2004, the state's agricultural productivity rose 2.3% annually and 3.0% per acre. By comparison national agricultural productivity rose less over the same period at 1.7% overall and 2.2% per acre.

According to the United States Department of Agriculture, from 1990 to 2004 (latest data), California's agricultural production rose 32% and on less farm land.

America has less farmland because it has not needed as much as before to serve its customers.

Of course, there has been substantial reduction of farmland close to some metropolitan areas, but overall the impact of urbanization nationally has not been substantial. For example, since 1950:

- The farmland reduction in largely rural downstate Illinois has been four times that of the vast former rural areas of metropolitan Chicago, which is home to the world's third most "sprawling" urban area, after New York and Tokyo.

- The farmland reduction in the Phoenix metropolitan area has been 6 *times* the expansion of urbanization.

In addition, the nation's agriculture is subsidized to the tune of more than $15 billion annually, which is strong evidence that more land is being farmed than is required. Subsidies increase the supply of virtually anything beyond its underlying demand. This can be illustrated by imagining how much less transit service there would be if it were not 80% subsidized. Suffice it to say, America is not threatened by "disappearing farmland."

America has less farmland because it has not needed as much as before to serve its customers. Thus, considerable farmland has been returned to a more natural state. Generally, this has got to be good for the environment. Land that is left to nature does not require fertilization, for example. The same interests that have frequently claimed that farmland has been disappearing also decry the loss of open space. In fact, the withdrawal of redundant farmland has produced considerable open space—call it open space sprawl.

If there is a serious threat to agriculture, it is from over-zealous regulation that has put farmers at risk.

The Cause of Farm Reduction

None of this has kept "disappearing farmland" from being a rallying cry among those who would construct Berlin Walls around the nation's urban areas. Yet the extent to which Bonnie Erbé of *Politics Daily* and National Public Radio embraced the fiction was surprising. Her "Vanishing Farmland: How It's Destabilizing America's Food Supply," was accompanied by "meant to indict" photograph of farm equipment next to new suburban housing.

Ms. Erbé's principal source was a web page from the American Farmland Trust, which seeks to conserve farm land. In its *California Agricultural Land Loss & Conservation: The Basic Facts*, the American Farmland Trust argues for more "efficient" (i.e. denser) urbanization and claims that, "One-sixth. . ." (17%) ". . . of the land urbanized since the Gold Rush . . . has been developed since 1990." That might be an impressive figure, if it were not that the state has added 7 million urban residents since 1990, which is one-fourth (25%) of all the urban population added since the Gold Rush and equal to the 1990 population of New York City.

It is worth noting that California has agricultural preservation measures already in place for farm owners and, finally, that no one can compel an unwilling farm owner to sell their land to a developer or anyone else (except perhaps a government agency through eminent domain).

In California, as elsewhere in the nation, urbanization has not been the principal cause of farm land reduction. According to the US Census of Agriculture, farmland declined in California from 2002 to 2007 by 2.2 million acres. That *5 year* reduction in farmland is approximately equal to the expansion of all California urban areas over the *50 years* between 1950 and 2000.

The Problems with Regulation

In the same document, the American Farmland Trust indicates support for the radical urban land regulations. Policies such as in Sacramento's *Blueprint* that significantly inflate the price of land, make housing less affordable. The agricultural, property and urban planning interests who would ration land for people and their houses have missed a larger target such as ultra-low density "ranchettes" favored by a small wealthy minority who live in the country, but are not farmers.

According to the US Department of Agriculture, rural, large lot residential development (non-agricultural) covered 40% *more* land than all of the nation's urbanization in 2000. These parcels represent "scattered single houses on large parcels, often 10 or more acres in size." Further, since 1980, the increase in this rural residential development has been one-third *greater* than the land area occupied by all of the urban areas in the nation with more than 1,000,000 population.

Finally, if there is a serious threat to agriculture, it is from over-zealous regulation that has put farmers at risk. Water reductions in the San Joaquin Valley—mostly the result of environmental demands—likely have taken more land out of production than any sprawl-happy developer.

The human footprint, as measured by the total urban and agricultural land has been declining for decades, both in the nation and California, where the greatest growth has occurred. The same is also true of Europe (EU-15), Canada and Australia, where all of the urbanization since the beginning of time does not equal the agricultural land recently taken out of production. Even in Japan, the human footprint has been reduced. It may be surprising, but human habitation and food production has returned considerable amounts of land to a more natural state in recent decades, while America's urban areas were welcoming 99% of all growth since 1950.

CHAPTER 3

What Effect Does Urban Sprawl Have on the Economy?

Somewhere to Live

The Economist

The Economist *is a weekly magazine in the United Kingdom that covers world news, business, politics, and other issues.*

Chandler and Maricopa are typical of the youthful, sprawling cities on the southern edge of Phoenix, Arizona. The thousands of stucco-walled houses with tiled roofs in Chandler's palm-tree-lined streets could have been stamped out by a machine that then moved on to produce the same sort of houses in Maricopa 17 miles to the south-west.

The Divergent Fates of Two Cities

Yet the two cities' economic fortunes have followed quite different paths. In 2000 Maricopa was just a dusty crossroads with 329 homes. The housing boom was its making. As in countless "exurbs" across America, lower-income families drove ever farther afield to find a house they could afford. Maricopa soon grew to over 15,000 homes. But when America's housing market collapsed, so did Maricopa's. Over a quarter of its houses have received a foreclosure notice, says RealtyTrac, a property consultancy. Howard Weinstein, a local landbroker, waves at a patch of lots in the desert which the bank seized from someone who bought them for $30,000 each: "At current house prices no builder would pay anything for these lots."

Chandler too has felt its share of pain as Arizona's housing boom crumbled; home prices are down by half and foreclosures have soared. But its cluster of high-tech employers, anchored by Intel, have weathered the recession better than most firms and are now enjoying a global rebound in business investment in technology. Builders are snapping up scraps of empty land near the city's centre.

Chandler's and Maricopa's divergent fates reflect the fact that as the crisis and recession reshape America's economic activity, they will also redraw its economic map. For most of the post-war period the South has been catching up with the rest of the country. Land there is cheaper and land-use regulation more permissive, making it a magnet for families seeking a house with a yard, even if it means long commutes from sprawling suburbs. In the sand states—Florida, Arizona, Nevada and California—these trends went into overdrive in the years leading up to the crisis.

A Shift in Migration

The rush for both sun and sprawl has now reversed, at least temporarily. Population growth has slowed in the suburbs and picked up in cities. During the recession four of the five states with the biggest job losses were in the sunbelt, led by Arizona, according to Moody's Economy.com. For the first time since the end of the second world war more people left Florida than moved in.

Some even predict that cities will regain economic leadership from suburbs.

Exactly the opposite happened in North Dakota. For only the second time since the 1970s more people are moving in than out and the population is now its highest since 1998. Enrolment at the high school in tiny Tioga is rising as locals who moved away years ago return with their children, and the principal frets that he now has to compete with the oil industry to hire janitors.

Internal migration has been slowed sharply by the fact that a quarter of homeowners with mortgages owe more than their home is worth, according to First American CoreLogic, making it difficult to move. Moreover, an economy shifting away from consumption and housing and towards exports of high-value goods and services will tend to benefit industries that cluster in metropolitan centres, in part because such firms draw on a common pool of intellectual talent. Software publishing, sound recording, film production and securities and commodities trading all form such clusters, note Bradford Jensen and Lori Kletzer in a report for the Peterson Institute. Seattle's share of employment in America's software industry, for example, is 18 times its share of population. By contrast, non-tradable services like retail banking and video rental do not show much clustering at all. New York City is reeling from the devastation visited on financial services but retains a leading role in other services, from media to architecture.

Some even predict that cities will regain economic leadership from suburbs. Richard Florida, an expert on urban planning at the University of Toronto, wrote in the *Atlantic* last year that the economy "no longer revolves around simply making and moving things. Instead, it depends on generating and transporting ideas. The places that thrive today are those with the highest velocity of ideas, the highest density of talented and creative people, the highest rate of metabolism," which are found in cities.

As long as Americans want to own homes, the South and suburban sprawl will retain a certain appeal.

Let's Hear It for the Suburbs

But that may be going too far. Powerful economic logic underpins the suburbs and car culture. The median commute by car, at 24 minutes, is half the median commute by public transport. Nathaniel Baum-Snow of Brown University has found that since 1960 residents and jobs have been moving to the suburbs at about the same rate. Cutbacks on highway construction will slow that trend but not reverse it.

Short-term trends seem as likely to benefit a city like Chandler as New York: it combines a suburb's ease of commuting and affordable housing with a city's clustering of workers with similar skills. Since Intel arrived in 1980, an infrastructure of suppliers and supporting industries has grown up around it. Air Products set up shop to deliver ultra-pure nitrogen, vital to chipmaking, to Intel down a two-foot-wide pipe. That pipe, in turn, attracted other semiconductor companies. Those companies and their suppliers have nurtured a pool of highly trained technical workers fed by two large state universities. Qualastat, which builds flexible circuits, recently announced it would move its headquarters to Chandler from Pennsylvania to be closer to a supply of engineers.

Chandler has all the things Intel looks for when deciding where to put a factory, says Brian Krzanich, Intel's general manager of manufacturing and operations: space, infrastructure, the transport links that enable it to ship completed wafers to other facilities in the country around the clock and, most important of all, a "pool of talent that's been here a long time".

It doesn't hurt, he adds, that a recent college graduate can more easily afford a home in Chandler than in the San Francisco bay area, where Intel is based. Still, Mr Krzanich gives warning that neither Chandler nor America can take Intel's presence for granted: "Other countries like China are climbing up the skillset. They're fighting fiercely for the same investment." Intel is now building its first fabrication plant outside the rich world—in China.

As long as Americans want to own homes, the South and suburban sprawl will retain a certain appeal. Eventually those foreclosed homes in Maricopa will be reoccupied. As Mr Weinstein, the landbroker, puts it, "in the 1990s Chandler felt like Maricopa does today. The only difference is the zip code and the decade."

Material World: How Peak Oil Pricked the Housing Bubble

Jason Mark

Jason Mark is editor of the environmental quarterly Earth Island Journal *and author of* Building the Green Economy: Success Stories from the Grassroots.

When, in the summer of 2009, the sociopath Bernie Madoff was sentenced to 150 years in prison, the news accounts proclaimed that Madoff had perpetrated the largest, longest Ponzi scheme in the history of the United States. How quickly we forget. Or—more to the point—how happy we are to let a good story take the place of hard truths. Just a season before Madoff's unmasking, the global economy had been driven to the brink of disaster by a much bigger swindle. It was a plot hiding in plain sight, at once more complex and more obvious, with many more perpetrators and far more victims. The scam was elegantly simple, leveraging the inexhaustible hopefulness of the American Dream against the warnings of our better judgment. Tens of millions of people were eager to buy into the idea that we could keep building homes far from any services or jobs, and that these properties would keep appreciating in value—forever. I like to call this particular Ponzi scheme "the US suburban housing market."

The contours of the housing bubble's rise and fall have become clearer from the vantage of the wreckage. For decades, city councils and county supervisors, ever eager for more property tax revenues, floated bonds to pay for the streets and sewers to accommodate home building—and then had to keep borrowing to fund even newer housing developments that would supply the tax base to pay off the previous loans. Homebuilders were more than happy to play the game. They constructed millions of homes on spec, even when the homes—their large size and far-out locations—were completely mismatched with the needs of US families, which were shrinking. With an excess supply of houses, someone had to gin up demand for all those lots. Enter an army of shifty mortgage companies and predatory lenders who helped sell homes to people who had no way to pay for them. In Washington, [then-chairman of the Federal Reserve] Alan Greenspan kept the party going by maintaining interest rates at all-time lows, igniting a debt binge. On Wall Street, financiers created all kinds of esoteric "investment vehicles" that shoveled even more credit into the maw of the real estate market. Loads of people got rich.

Then the music stopped. Since the end of 2006, nearly 6.5 million homes have been lost to foreclosure and more than 4 million homeowners are "seriously delinquent" on their mortgage payments. Roughly a quarter of homes in the United States are underwater; the value of the property is less than what's owed on the mortgage. The single family home, once a family's most important asset, has become a financial liability for tens of millions of people.

If American suburbia was raised on easy credit, it was suckled on cheap gasoline.

By now a shelf's worth of books have been written about how this came to pass. The insider accounts offer a perverse tale of how the "false economy"—the Wall Street whirlwind of credit default swaps and mortgage derivatives and wanton speculation—kneecapped the real economy—the place where people make goods and services that have actual uses. The investigative exposés are essential reading for anyone who wants to understand how late-stage capitalism works.

And yet they fail to tell the whole story. I have read a number of those books, and I looked in vain through their pages for a phrase that I suspected would be there: "rising gas prices." This seems to me a stunning oversight. The mainstream narratives of the real estate collapse neglect a crucial fact. They don't note that everyone involved—from the Goldman Sachs vampires, to the boiler room loan sharks, to local homebuilders and federal officials—shared the assumption that gasoline would stay cheap enough to subsidize houses in the middle of nowhere.

Perhaps it's because [philosopher Karl] Marx is unfashionable among the reporters who cover the financial markets, but the exposés all miss an essential fact: Our economy remains grounded in material resources. It has become common to compare the 2007–2008 meltdown with the Crash of 1929 or the Great Panic of 1873. The comparison is useful, to a point. There's an important difference, though. During the earlier contagions of panic a mentality of scarcity overshadowed a genuine abundance of natural wealth. Think of the Depression-era farmers pouring out good milk because there were no buyers for it. But the age of abundance is over. Today we are in the midst of actual scarcity, at least when it comes to the essential material of our civilization—oil.

As long as Americans want to own homes, the South and suburban sprawl will retain a certain appeal.

If American suburbia was raised on easy credit, it was suckled on cheap gasoline. To borrow from the language of accountants, our oil addiction is what you could call an "off-balance-sheet risk." Now that risk is being reckoned. The US economy slammed into a brick wall because, in part, the housing market had reached the limits of growth. There was no more cheap fuel to keep it expanding.

The far-flung reaches of suburbia also have reached the limits of believability. It turns out that a 3,000-square-foot home a one-hour drive from work isn't really such a bargain—not when gas is $4/gallon, not when transportation is the second biggest cost for the average American household. Real utility has corrected imagined value: There's no use in spending your life savings on an oversized shelter if you can't afford to even get there. The $100 weekly gas bill has dealt a fatal blow to the suspension of disbelief on which the real estate Ponzi scheme always relied.

Elementary geology: the fossil fuels on which we have built our entire civilization won't last forever. The Peak Oil-ers who are determined to remind us of this law of nature have been waiting with undisguised glee for the day when the price of oil would catch up to the suburbs. James Howard Kunstler, the most acerbic of the Peak Oil contingent, calls suburbia "the greatest misallocation of resources in world history" and "a living arrangement that had no future." It appears that we've arrived at that dead-end.

Total global production of "conventional" petroleum reached its all time high in 2005 and since then has remained steady—evidence that the laws of supply and demand will force some version of a petroleum plateau rather than a sharp peak. There's still plenty of oil left on the planet. That is, as long as we're prepared to grub for the deposits of hard-to-get, "unconventional" fuels under the boreal forests of Canada, locked in the savannahs of Venezuela, or hidden in the deep waters off Brazil. Even if we do—and fry the globe in the process—the era of cheap and easy oil is over. And since cheap and easy has always been the dominant ideology of suburbia, the suburbs (or at least their farthest fringes) are seeing the end of their best days.

Take a look at the numbers. In 2001, when the Federal Reserve opened the credit spigot that led to the mortgage mania, gas was at a national average of $1.50 a gallon. By the spring of 2007—as many adjustable rate mortgages were resetting at higher rates—the price of gas had risen to $3 a gallon. It might be hard to imagine that a doubling of monthly fuel costs would cause a wave of defaults. But consider this: In 2005, two-thirds of borrowers at Countrywide, one of the nation's biggest mortgage firms, put no down payment on their homes. That same year, 29 percent of all mortgages in the US were negative-amortization loans, taken out by people who had so little cash that they were willing to tack their interest payments onto the principal. And they were taking out those loans even as their incomes were stagnating or declining.

The homes out in the exurbs were a "bargain" only as long [as] gas stayed inexpensive.

To break it all down: Millions of people went into debt buying homes they couldn't afford and, since they were nearly broke already, they had no way to cover a spike in their gas bills. Something had to give. For families spending a quarter of their earnings on transportation, the choice came down to their house or their second home—the car.

The evidence of the collapse is all around us: The weedy lots in the California subdivisions; Florida's empty McMansions that have been stripped for copper wiring; the newly built Las Vegas neighborhoods that are uninhabited. "Gated Ghettos" is how one dark-witted real estate agent described these places to the *Los Angeles Times*. According to the US Census Bureau, the suburban poverty rate is at its highest level since 1967, when the government began keeping such statistics. Christopher Leinberger, a fellow at the Brookings Institution, has written that the outer ring suburbs are poised to become America's next slums, "characterized by poverty, crime, and decay."

A few studies show how this is happening. A 2008 white paper from a group called CEOs for Cities notes that "as gas prices sustained [a] higher level and then increased in 2006 and 2007, first to $2.50 and then to $3, housing price inflation collapsed, and, indeed turned negative." The suburbs on the farthest edge were hit hardest. "Our analysis . . . finds that prices have declined most in the most distant neighborhoods," the paper says. Another study by the Center for Neighborhood Technology confirms this trend. The center mapped every foreclosure in the Chicago area from 1998 to 2009 and found that the farther houses were from downtown, the higher the rate of foreclosures. As gas prices kept climbing, the "drive-until-you-qualify" mentality hit a roadblock. The homes out in the exurbs were a "bargain" only as long [as] gas stayed inexpensive.

Of course, coincidence doesn't equal causality. Did a spike in gasoline prices provide the spark that engulfed an over-leveraged debt system? Or were financial shenanigans the catalyst that collapsed a structure overdependent on fossil fuels? As Alex Steffens, an ecological urbanist, put it to me: "The answer is probably D: All of the Above."

What matters now is that persistently high gas prices (holding steady between $3.50 and $4 a gallon through much of 2011) are serving as a drag on the economy. The recovery remains stalled, and many economists agree that the weakness in the housing market is a major cause, as depressed home prices dampen spenders' confidence. CEOs for Cities reports: "The new calculus of higher gas prices may have permanently reshaped urban housing markets." Arthur C. Nelson, a professor at the University of Utah and an expert on urban development, has done the math to prove the point. He figures that, nationally, there is a surplus of 25 million homes and large lots. Supply for many properties outstrips demand. People aren't interested in living on the suburban fringe anymore.

The Brookings Institution's Leinberger pointed out to me that, in 2000, big homes on large lots outside of Washington, DC were worth 25 percent more than townhouses in Dupont Circle, in the heart of the capital. By 2010, the urban townhouse was worth 70 percent more than the house in what Leinberger calls "horsey country." "The lines crossed," he says. "There has been, in essence, a structural shift." Our cities are transitioning toward a European model, where the affluent live in the central core while the poor, ethnic minorities, and recent immigrants are shunted off to the hinterlands.

Someone is spending $700 to $800 a month just for fuel for one car, if they have an SUV.

Leinberger told me he doesn't believe that high gas prices are driving this trend, but rather accelerating it. For families who were the last to buy into the outer ring suburbs—the latecomers to the Ponzi scheme—it makes little difference. They are still seeing a decline in their assets, their world turned inside out. The suburbs, once imagined as a refuge, have become more like a trap. To be living in a home that's underwater is just another way of saying that you've been shipwrecked and stranded.

Few places exemplify the suburban predicament as well as Stockton, California, a "city" of 300,000 people slung along the banks of the San Joaquin River. A hundred years ago, the place was an important inland port that transported Central Valley harvests down to the San Francisco Bay. Today, the town's elegant Magnolia District is a remnant of that era of natural wealth. But most of Stockton—which doubled in population since 1980—has outgrown its functionality. There are still jobs to be found in agriculture. For undocumented Mexicans, poorly paid work in the fields; for dudes with a high school diploma, maybe a forklift gig at the Big Ag warehouses. Aside from that, there's little local industry. Many

Stockton residents spend a lot of their time commuting: either crossing the Altamont Pass to get to work in Silicon Valley or driving 50 miles north to fill one of the dwindling number of government jobs in Sacramento. Everyone else peddles services to each other, or sells stuff made in China.

One out of five people in Stockton is unemployed. The city routinely ranks among the top ten communities for home foreclosures and as many as 75 percent of properties are underwater. *Forbes* magazine has dubbed it the "most miserable" place in America.

As the era of scarcity lengthens, Stockton's vulnerability to costly gasoline has become obvious. "If you live over here, gas price is everything," Randy Thomas, a real estate agent, told me. "It's killing us. It's crazy. Someone is spending $700 to $800 a month just for fuel for one car, if they have an SUV. And a lot of people are charging it. The gas on their credit card bills work into their debt-to-income ratio."

Whenever it comes, the recovery will not be a restoration of the cheap-oil status quo. It will be more of an evolution to a different way of life.

Thomas tells me that "people are going to start making bigger sacrifices for energy." In a place built on the commute, everyone gets hit in some way. The affluent decide they have to pull the kids out of private school. The middle classes are forced to give up the dinners out and the yearly vacation. The poor are shifted onto the rolls of the local charities. "People might think that this just hit the low income," a Stockton developer named Carol Ornelas says. "Nu-uh. This happened across the board. This is the whole middle class that is collapsing."

A gloom has settled over the place. For many people, success has been redefined to simply mean survival, Thomas says. Ornelas says, "This is the worst it's ever been, and I've been here 26 years." Food pantries are struggling to keep up with a spike in demand; charities are having to help people meet their healthcare and utility bills. "There's no end in sight, things are going to get worse, and families are afraid," a long-time Stockton social worker named Elvira Ramirez told me. "Families—I don't want to say despair—but they don't know where to turn to."

Still, optimism is the signature American character trait, and the people of Stockton are trying to stay hopeful that eventually the situation will turn around. "We have to not be hopeless," Ramirez says. "We have to do the best we can." For the most remote neighborhoods of Stockton, "the best they can do" will involve a wholesale rethinking of what suburbia is supposed to look like. Whenever it comes, the recovery will not be a restoration of the cheap-oil status quo. It will be more of an evolution to a different way of life. Professor Nelson imagines that many houses in suburbia will be converted from single-family homes to multiple-family dwellings. Big houses will become apartment buildings; private yards will be turned into commons. To survive what could be $8 a gallon gas by 2020 (if current growth rates continue), people would have no option but to pile up. Think of it as the remodeling of the American Dream.

The work of rebuilding an outdated world will be grueling.

And what of those places that might be unsuitable even for redesigning? They will be abandoned. If that sounds overstated, just take in this fact: After being the fastest-growing regions of the country for decades, the Sun Belt is beginning to experience an out-migration. In the last three years, Florida has experienced its first net migration loss since the 1940s. Same with Las Vegas. Arizona is just barely holding on. "If nobody can buy or sell their homes, there's going to be a stagnancy," a demographer at the Brookings Institution told *The New York Times* when the migration statistics were published.

Much of what we've built, it turns out is worthless.

In classic tragic form, much of this pain could have been avoided if only wisdom had overcome hubris. For decades, a minority chorus of designers, urban planners, environmentalists, and a few enlightened leaders warned about the consequences of building homes for the sake of building homes— "the ideology of the cancer cell," in the unforgettable words of Edward Abbey. As they've been saying, we know how to build better and, given what we've already built, how to retrofit. We can turn urban brownfields into high-density neighborhoods that combine housing, shopping, and services. We can pull out a lane of traffic and make rapid transit bus routes. The suburban garages can become in-law units. The freeway right-of-ways can get turned into light rail corridors. The golf courses might become community farms. "Forget about a dream house," writes Nick Aster, editor of the website TriplePundit. "Think about a dream neighborhood."

These ideas are off-the-shelf and shovel-ready. Which is not to say that implementing them will be easy. Not when thousands of homeowners associations around the US prohibit rooftop solar panels and backyard clotheslines. Not in places where neighborhoods don't even have sidewalks. The work of rebuilding an outdated world will be grueling. The transition—what Peak Oil-er Kunstler has dubbed "The Long Emergency"—will demand a whole new valuation of things. In a world restored to limits, our priorities will change. Craftsmanship will once again be worth more than cleverness. Useful skills, the ability to build and grow things, will take precedence over the exchange of complex services. Place will become more important than size.

As we are learning the hard way, this process will be painful. Our best hope is that it will be cathartic, too. The meltdown of the housing market, as horrible as it has been, can serve as a long overdue wakeup call that, despite our dreams, we remain tethered to the natural resources of Earth. It's a reminder that we can't pull riches out of thin air. It's proof that our society's wealth always has, and always will, come from the body of the world.

The Next Real Estate Boom

Patrick C. Doherty and Christopher B. Leinberger

Patrick C. Doherty is deputy director of the National Security Studies Program and director of the Smart Strategy Initiative at the New America Foundation. Christopher B. Leinberger is a nonresident senior fellow at the Brookings Institution, a professor at the University of Michigan, and a real estate developer.

What if there were a new economic engine for the United States that would put our people back to work without putting the government deeper in debt? What if that economic engine also improved our international competitiveness, reduced greenhouse gases, and made the American people healthier?

At a minimum, it would sound a lot better than any of the current offers on the table: stimulus from the liberals, austerity from the conservatives, and the president's less-than-convincing plan for a little stimulus, a little austerity, and a little bit of a clean-energy economy.

The potential for just such an economic renaissance is a lot more plausible than many would imagine. At the heart of this opportunity are the underappreciated implications of a massive demographic convergence. In short, the two largest demographic groups in the country, the baby boomers and their children—together comprising half the population—want homes and commercial space in neighborhoods that do not exist in anywhere near sufficient quantity. Fixing this market failure, unleashing this latent demand, and using it to put America back to work could be accomplished without resorting to debt-building stimulus or layoff-inducing austerity. At least for the moment, Washington has an opportunity to speed up private investment for public good and launch what could be a period of long-lasting prosperity. It is a market-driven way to make the economic recovery sustainable while addressing many of the most serious problems of our time: the health care crisis, climate change, over-reliance on oil from countries with terrorist ties, and an overextended military.

Real estate has caused two of the last three recessions, including the Great Recession we've just gone through. That is because real estate (housing, commercial, and industrial) and the infrastructure that supports real estate (transportation, sewer, electricity, and so on) represent 35 percent of the economy's asset base. When real estate crashes, the economy goes into a tailspin. To speed up the economic recovery now slowly underway, the real estate sector *must* get back into the game, just as it played a central role in the economic recoveries of past recessions. (Real estate also kept the high-tech recession in the early 2000s from being as serious as it might have been.) The United States will be condemned to high unemployment and sluggish growth if 35 percent of our asset base is not engaged. And hundreds of billions of dollars in potential investment capital is on the sidelines, waiting for the right market signals to be deployed.

The Great Recession has highlighted a fundamental change in what consumers do want: homes in central cities and closer-in suburbs.

We're unlikely, however, to see a real estate recovery based on a continuation of the type of development that has driven the industry for the past few generations: low-density, car-dependent suburbs growing out of cornfields at the edge of metropolitan areas. That's because there is now a massive oversupply of such suburban fringe development, brought on by decades of policy favoring it—including heavy government subsidies for extending roads, sewers, and utilities into undeveloped land. Houses on the exurban fringe of several large metro areas have typically lost more than twice as much value as metro areas as a whole since the mid-decade peak. Many of those homes are now priced below the cost of the materials that went into building them, which means that their owners have no financial incentive to invest in their upkeep. Under such conditions, whole neighborhoods swiftly decline and turn into slums. This happened in many inner-city neighborhoods in the 1960s, and we're seeing evidence of it in many exurban neighborhoods today. The *Los Angeles Times* reports that in one gated community in Hemet, east of L.A., McMansions with granite countertops and vaulted ceilings are being rented to poor families on Section 8 vouchers; according to the *Washington Examiner*, similar homes in Germantown, Maryland, outside Washington, D.C., are being converted to boarding houses.

Many hope that when the economy recovers, demand will pick up, inventories of empty homes will be whittled down, and the traditional suburban development machine will lumber back to life. But don't bet on it. Demand for standard-issue suburban housing is going down, not up, a trend that was apparent even before the crash. In 2006, Arthur C. Nelson, now at the University of Utah, estimated in the *Journal of the American Planning Association* that there will be 22 million unwanted large-lot suburban homes by 2025.

Meanwhile, the Great Recession has highlighted a fundamental change in what consumers *do* want: homes in central cities and closer-in suburbs where one can walk to stores and mass transit. Such "walkable urban" real estate has experienced less than half the average decline in price from the housing peak. Ten years ago, the highest property values per square foot in the Washington, D.C., metro area were in car-dependent suburbs like Great Falls, Virginia. Today, walkable city neighborhoods like Dupont Circle command the highest per-square-foot prices, followed by dense suburban neighbor-hoods near subway stops in places like Bethesda, Maryland, and Arlington, Virginia. Similarly, in Denver, property values in the high-end car-dependent suburb of Highland Ranch are now lower than those in the redeveloped LoDo neighborhood near downtown. These trend lines have been evident in many cities for a number of years; at some point during the last de-cade, the lines crossed. The last time the lines crossed was in the 1960—and they were heading the opposite direction.

There are some obvious reasons for the growing demand for walkable neighborhoods: ever-worsening traffic conges-tion, memories of the 2008 spike in gasoline prices, and the fact that many cities have become more attractive places to live thanks to falling crime rates and the replacement of heavy industries with cleaner, higher-end service and professional economies.

But the biggest factor, one that will quickly pick up speed in the next few years, is demographic. The baby boomers and their children, the millennial generation, are looking for places to live and work that reflect their current desires and life needs. Boomers are downsizing as their children leave home while the millennials, or generation Y, are setting out on their careers with far different housing needs and preferences. Both of these huge demographic groups want something that the U.S. housing market is not currently providing: small one- to three-bedroom homes in walkable, transit-oriented, economi-cally dynamic, and job-rich neighborhoods.

The baby boom generation, defined as those born between 1946 and 1964, remains the largest demographic bloc in the United States. At approximately 77 million Americans, they are fully one-quarter of the population. With the leading edge of the boomers now approaching sixty-five years old, the group is finding that their suburban houses are too big. Their child-rearing days are ending, and all those empty rooms have to be heated, cooled, and cleaned, and the unused backyard maintained. Suburban houses can be socially isolating, especially as aging eyes and slower reflexes make driving everywhere less comfortable. Freedom for many in this generation means living in walkable, accessible communities with convenient transit linkages and good public services like libraries, cultural activities, and health care. Some boomers are drawn to cities. Others prefer to stay in the suburbs but want to trade in their large-lot single-family detached homes on cul-de-sacs for smaller-lot single-family homes, townhouses, and condos in or near burgeoning suburban town centers.

An epic amount of money will pour into the real estate market as a result of population growth and demographic confluence.

Generation Y has a different story. The second-largest generation in the country, born between 1977 and 1994 and numbering 76 million, millennials are leaving the nest. They may sometimes fall back into the nest, but eventually they find a place of their own for the first time. Following the lead of their older cousins, the much smaller generation X (those born between 1965 and 1976), a high proportion of millennials have a taste for vibrant, compact, and walkable communities full of economic, social, and recreational opportunities. Their aspirations have been informed by *Friends* and *Sex and the City*, shows set in walkable urban places, as opposed to their parents' mid-century imagery of *Leave It to Beaver* and *Brady Bunch*, set in the drivable suburbs. Not surprisingly, fully 77 percent of millennials plan to live in America's urban cores. The largest group of millennials began graduating from college in 2009, and if this group rents for the typical three years, from 2013 to 2018 there will be more aspiring first-time homebuyers in the American marketplace than ever before— and only half say they will be looking for drivable suburban homes. Reinforcing that trend, housing industry experts, like

Todd Zimmerman of Zimmerman/Volk Associates, believe that this generation is more likely to plant roots in walkable urban areas and force local government to fix urban school districts rather than flee to the burbs for their schools.

The convergence of these two trends is the biggest demographic event since the baby boom itself. The first wave of boomers will be sixty-five in 2011. The largest number of millennials reaches age twenty-two in 2012. With the last of the boomers hitting sixty-five in 2029, this convergence is set to last decades. In addition to the generational convergence, the Census Bureau estimates that America is going to grow from 310 million people today to 440 million by 2050.

An epic amount of money will pour into the real estate market as a result of population growth and demographic confluence. To be sure, unemployment and stagnant wages have eroded people's buying power. Boomers have suffered steep declines in the value of their current homes and 401(k)s, and young people are leaving college with ever-larger student loan debts.

But Americans of all ages have saved and paid off debts since the recession began, and average household balance sheets should be significantly healthier five years from now. In addition, 85 percent of the new households formed between now and 2025 will be single individuals or couples with no children at home; unburdened by child-rearing expenses, they will have more income available for housing (and less desire to spend it tending big backyards).

Most importantly, the very act of moving to more walkable neighborhoods will free families from the expense of buying, fueling, and maintaining the two or more cars they typically need to get around in auto-dependent suburbs. Households in drivable suburban neighborhoods devote on average 24 percent of their income to transportation; those in walkable neighborhoods spend about 12 percent. The difference is equal to half of what a typical household spends on health care—nationally, that amounts to $700 billion a year in total, according to Scott Bernstein of the Center for Neighborhood Technology. Put another way, dropping one car out of the typical household budget can allow that family to afford a $100,000 larger mortgage.

[Chronic diseases] would be substantially reduced if Americans move into higher-density, transit-friendly neighborhoods in which more walking is built into their daily routine.

The burgeoning demand for homes in walkable communities has the potential to reshape the American landscape and rejuvenate its economy as profoundly as the wave of suburbanization after World War II did. If anything, today's opportunity is larger. The returning veterans and their spouses represented approximately 20 percent of the American population at that time; the current demographic convergence—77 million boomers plus 76 million millennials—comprises nearly 50 percent.

In the postwar years, America pushed its built environment outward, beyond the central cities, creating millions of new construction jobs and new markets for cars and appliances—a virtuous cycle of commerce that helped power American prosperity for decades (until, of course, it went too far, leading to the oversupply of exurban development that is acting as deadweight on the current recovery). The coming demographic convergence will push construction inward, accelerating the rehabilitation of cities and forcing existing car-dependent suburbs to develop more compact, walkable, and transit-friendly neighborhoods if they want to keep property values up and attract tomorrow's homebuyers. All this rebuilding could spur millions of new construction jobs. But more importantly, if done right, with "smart growth" zoning codes that reward energy efficiency, it would create new markets for power-conserving materials and appliances, providing American designers and manufacturers with experience producing the kinds of green products world markets will increasingly want.

In addition to fueling long-term economic growth, the new demand for walkable neighborhoods could provide other benefits. One of the biggest drivers of rising health care costs is the expansion of chronic diseases like obesity, diabetes, and heart disease—conditions exacerbated by the sedentary lifestyles of our car-dependent age. All would be substantially reduced if Americans move into higher-density, transit-friendly neighborhoods in which more walking is built into their daily routine.

The potential environmental benefits are equally profound. A study conducted by the Natural Resources Defense Council concluded that simply conforming new construction to smart growth standards would reduce carbon emissions 10 percent within ten years, more than half the target set by the president and the stalled climate legislation. Similarly, the U.S. Green Building Council estimates that new sustainable developments could reduce water consumption by 40 percent, energy use by up to 50 percent, and solid waste by 70 percent.

We can reap these economic, health, and environmental benefits if the real estate market is allowed to follow the demand preferences of consumers. But that's easier said than done. Markets don't exist in a vacuum. They operate within rules and incentives set by governments. The rules and incentives that guide today's real estate market were designed, for the most part, more than a half century ago to fit the demands of the postwar-era Americans who were looking for new homes with yards outside overcrowded cities in which to raise their families. For many years the government-insured mortgages provided to millions of GIs were regulated in such a way that they could only be used to buy newly constructed homes, not to purchase or rehab existing homes—an incentive that strongly biased growth away from cities and toward the suburbs. Cheap rural land outside cities became accessible and valuable to developers thanks to the building of the interstate highway system, 90 percent funded by the federal government. Using federal matching grants, suburban municipalities extended water, sewer, and electric lines to new subdivisions, charging developers and homeowners a fraction of the real costs of those extensions. Municipalities also crafted zoning codes, often in response to federal regulations that essentially mandated low-density development.

Today, even though consumer preferences have changed, most of the old rules and subsidies remain in place. For instance, federal transportation funding formulas, combined with the old-school thinking of many state departments of transportation, continue to favor the building of new roads and widening of highways—infrastructure that supports low-density, car-dependent development—over public transit systems that are the foundation for most compact, walkable neighborhoods. When developers do propose to build denser projects, with narrower streets and apartments above retail space, they often run up against zoning codes that make such building illegal. Consequently, few compact, walkable neighborhoods have been built relative to demand, and real estate prices in them have often been bid up to astronomical heights. This gives the impression that such neighborhoods are only popular with the affluent, when in fact millions of middle-class Americans would likely jump at the opportunity to live in them.

To meet this broad new demand, however, requires that entire metropolitan regions work together to chart a common vision for their communities. When that happens, all kinds of Americans, and not just coastal elites, choose walkable, transit-based growth.

Consider the recent experience of Utah, a state that voted 63 percent for John McCain and Sarah Palin [in 2010]. In

1997, in anticipation of the 2002 Winter Olympics in Salt Lake City, a coalition of local CEOs [chief executive officers], elected leaders, developers, farmers' associations, conservation advocates, and urban planners put together a process of public meetings to get citizens involved in developing a strategy to accommodate greater Salt Lake City's fast-paced growth in a fiscally and environmentally sustainable way. That process, dubbed "Envision Utah," led to a blueprint for development in the four-county region. The plan largely rejects further suburban sprawl in favor of a "quality growth strategy" of dense walkable neighborhoods built around transit stops.

The public, then, has made its desire for transit-oriented growth quite clear, and governments at the local and metropolitan levels have begun to respond.

The first step was the building of a seventeen-mile, twenty-three-station light rail line in Salt Lake City called TRAX. The line was highly controversial; many predicted it would be an underutilized boondoggle. But when the first phase opened in 1999, TRAX proved an immediate hit with the public—eventually some trains became so crowded with riders that their doors couldn't close. In 2000 and 2006, voters approved tax increases to expand the system, including increased reach to several outlying suburbs, twenty-six miles of new light rail track, forty additional station stops, and eighty-eight miles of heavier commuter rail, reaching as far as Provo. Meanwhile, mixed residential-commercial developments have been constructed around existing stations in places like the formerly industrial suburb of Murray City.

Locally financed transit expansions are also underway in such wide-ranging places as St. Louis, Denver, Los Angeles, Montgomery, Alabama, and Broward County, Florida. From 2004 to 2009, 67 percent of light rail ballot measures passed. In 2008, the election year defined by the financial crisis, 87 percent of transit measures passed. In Seattle, a 2008 measure saw sponsors actually eliminate road funding so that the thirty-four-mile extension of the light rail system would pass.

The public, then, has made its desire for transit-oriented growth quite clear, and governments at the local and metropolitan levels have begun to respond. At the federal level, however, the policy machinery remains on autopilot, supporting a sprawl-based growth model that is beyond broken. What we need to do should be obvious: replace old federal rules and incentives that hamper the market's ability to meet changing needs and preferences for housing with new ones that don't, thus helping to rejuvenate the American economy. But these new policies will have to be produced in a political environment that, unlike in the postwar years, is hostile to government actions that add considerably to the federal deficit. And they need to be written quickly: the peak of the convergence is only three years away, and the economy needs a sustainable base from which to grow more quickly now.

Throughout human history, transportation has determined the pattern of real estate development, and so the place to begin is federal transportation policy. Fortunately, next year [2011] Congress will probably reauthorize the giant transportation law that determines most federal infrastructure spending—which, tellingly enough, is still commonly referred to in Washington as "the highway bill." This will provide a golden opportunity to change federal policy in several fundamental ways. First, the biases in federal matching grants that favor roads and highways over every other type of infrastructure (sidewalks, bike paths, mass transit, and so on) must end. Second, the grants should be "scored" based on their economic, environmental, and social equity impacts—in particular, on the degree to which proposed transportation projects minimize travel times and distances for residents and enable compact, walkable, energy-efficient, and affordable development. Third, metro areas should be required, and given funding, to do what greater Salt Lake City did: create a blueprint for future growth. Those blueprints should then help guide which specific infrastructure projects get federal funding. In effect, this will shift the power to shape growth patterns away from congressional appropriators and state departments of transportation and to local citizens and local elected officials. And it will help ensure that actual consumer demand drives the process, rather than the current combination of antiquated federal funding formulas, congressional earmarks, and offstage machinations of conventional developers.

Many liberals might want Washington to cover most of the costs of this new infrastructure. That's unlikely to happen in the current political and fiscal environment. Nor, frankly, is it necessary, or even healthy. Instead, scarce federal dollars should be used to attract private dollars, of which there are plenty. The Investment Company Institute reports that institutional investors are keeping a relatively stable $1.8 trillion in money market funds because money managers see no good long-term investment vehicles. A similar amount is sitting in the coffers of non-financial corporations.

The Obama administration has proposed one way to tap some of these private dollars: create an "infrastructure bank" that would leverage several private dollars for every federal dollar invested to build a project. In return, the bank and private investors would receive, say, a dedicated locally raised future tax revenue source.

Another approach would be to revive a practice from the past. A hundred years ago, virtually every city of 5,000 or more had an extensive network of streetcars. These systems were typically not publicly owned. Instead, real estate developers, often in partnership with electric utilities, built and ran them, even paying municipal governments to rent the right-of-way. The developers made their money not from fares, which barely covered operations, but from the increased land values that the trolley extensions made possible. There's no reason why similar deals can't be negotiated today to fund various kinds of mass transit. In fact, the process has already begun in a few places. Developers are helping to pay for the extension of the Washington, D.C., metro rail to Dulles airport, while Microsoft cofounder Paul Allen's real estate company and other property owners participated in the funding of the streetcar to his substantial property holdings just north of downtown Seattle. The federal government can help make such arrangements much more common by offering partial guarantees of the debt floated to build transit infrastructure.

The truth is that federal housing policy can make only a modest dent in the affordability problem. As we've seen, what really drives development is transportation policy.

Another way Washington can encourage walkable neighborhoods is through reforms of Fannie Mae and Freddie Mac. These two government-sponsored mortgage guarantors and underwriters went bankrupt and were taken over by the U.S. government-in large part because they overinvested in homes on the suburban fringe. But in recent years Fannie Mae has been experimenting with an interesting new product: "location efficient mortgages." Instead of relying solely on credit score and income to determine whether a borrower qualifies for a mortgage, these loans use electronic map systems to take into account how much homeowners will have to pay for transportation. Research by Scott Bernstein of the Center for Neighborhood Technology suggests that location efficient mortgages may have lower default rates than conventional Fannie Mae loans. If that finding proves true, then it makes sense to expand the program, and to apply the same concept to household energy savings: Fannie, Freddie, and HUD's [US Department of Housing and Urban Development] Federal Housing Administration should factor in the savings from more energy-efficient homes and retrofits. And all these products should be available for more types of construction than just the single-family detached house.

In the past, big shifts in real estate patterns, from suburbanization to gentrification, have often made the lives of the poor considerably worse. To make sure that doesn't happen as we move toward more walkable communities, federal action will also be needed. The Obama administration took a first step earlier this year by announcing that location efficiency will be a criterion for $3.25 billion in competitive HUD housing grants. That means that at least some walkable developments will be built to include housing for lower-income families, and more can be done along these lines using existing federal housing programs such as the Low-Income Housing Tax Credit.

But the truth is that federal housing policy can make only a modest dent in the affordability problem. As we've seen, what really drives development is transportation policy, and so the real lever of change is, again, the upcoming transportation bill. The bill should offer state and local governments a clear choice: if they want federal dollars for light rail and other transit systems, they must ensure that citizens at all income levels reap the benefits. That means changing local zoning codes to mandate that a portion of the housing in transit-oriented developments—say, 15 percent—be reserved for lower-income families. It also means that local jurisdictions need to remove ordinances that act as barriers to affordable housing-an idea long championed by many conservatives, including the late [politician] Jack Kemp. For instance, empty nesters ought to have the right to rent out unused bedrooms or turn part of their homes into separate rental units. Doing so is illegal in most municipalities today.

Ultimately, the biggest barrier to affordability is insufficient supply: homes in walkable, transit-oriented neighborhoods cost too much because there are not enough of them to satisfy the growing market demand. What's needed, then, is a supply-side solution: build more such neighborhoods.

Can a set of policies like these ever get through Congress? After all, Republicans have long been ideologically hostile to mass transit. With their base now predominantly in exurban and rural America, most GOP lawmakers will look with skepticism, even disdain, at proposals to use government in ways that benefit cities and closer-in suburbs that tend to elect Democrats. And many Americans who live in rural or exurban areas feel the scorn that too many educated urbanites express for their lifestyle, and reflect that scorn right back.

Yet, as Utah shows, conservative Americans can rally behind mass transit when all the advantages are pointed out and the hidden costs of sprawl made clear. The threats to family life posed by long commutes and auto dependency are a building issue among evangelical Christians. Conservatives are often among the most acute critics of federal highway subsidies and the way they insulate consumers from the real cost of driving. The late Paul Weyrich, cofounder of the Heritage Foundation, served on Amtrak's board and was an outspoken champion of passenger rail. As William Lind recently argued in the *American Conservative* magazine, it was hardly a triumph of free enterprise that America's convenient and affordable streetcar and passenger rail systems, most of them privately owned, were put out of business by government-subsidized and -owned highways.

In the wake of the Great Recession there is also another huge pocketbook force at work: however they might lean ideologically, the best hope suburbanites have for reversing their depressed home values is for mass transit lines to be extended in their communities. Though not every suburb can be saved in this way, for many it represents the most practical long-term solution to their dilemma.

Ultimately, the strongest argument for these policies—one conservatives and liberals ought to be able to agree on—is that they would allow the moribund real estate market to function again, and in so doing would give the economy a dose of healthy growth. Indeed, assuming that a decisive package like the one above is passed, the private sector, awash in capital, may anticipate the demand about to be unleashed in our markets and start investing in real estate again. That is what happened in downtown Portland, Oregon, when a proposed $50 million streetcar led to $3.5 billion of private-sector development, much of it *before* the streetcar was built. America will be back in business. And good business is good politics.

But leading the transition to sustainability is also a strategic imperative for the United States. China and India need to figure out how to accommodate 700 million of their countrymen who will leave the villages and enter the cities over the next forty years. That's more than twice the total American population. China is already building at a pace that will allow it to have 221 cities with more than 1 million residents—the U.S. has nine. The competition for energy and raw materials like copper, lumber, and steel under a business-as-usual scenario is extraordinary and will result only in increased levels of strategic conflict in the decades ahead, as recent congressional hearings on "strategic minerals" attests. By making a decisive shift and embracing sustainable communities, innovative American firms will have the domestic markets they need to develop and deliver the super-efficient products and services that will keep America secure and, through increased exports, help build our economy while reducing our trade imbalance.

Admittedly, the road to sustainability only begins with how we build and rebuild our communities. In addition to the ideas discussed here, there is much more we need to do to address the energy and material intensity of our economy in ways that will lead to better jobs, higher wages, reduced deficits, and greater national security. But at a time when the American people need a plan for long-term prosperity, and because real estate absorbs so much of our wealth, it is essential that we focus on pushing on the door unlocked by our demographic inheritance: the two largest population groups, half of our population, want communities that the market is not delivering due to out-of-date subsidies and policies.

The bottom line is this: despite the protests of orthodox adherents to liberal and conservative fiscal policy, it is now possible to unleash latent private-sector demand by implementing reforms that will end our subsidies to sprawl and focus our nation on sustainability. Neither stimulus nor austerity, this approach would provide a new economic engine for America that can set us on a secure and prosperous path for years to come.

Job Sprawl Leads to Poverty in the Suburbs

Steven Raphael and Michael A. Stoll

Steven Raphael is professor of public policy at the University of California, Berkeley. Michael A. Stoll is associate professor of public policy in the School of Public Affairs and associate director of the Center for the Study of Urban Poverty at the University of California, Los Angeles; he is also a nonresident senior fellow in the Metropolitan Policy Program at the Brookings Institution.

In nearly all U.S. metropolitan areas, jobs have been moving to the suburbs for several decades. In the largest metropolitan areas between 1998 and 2006, jobs shifted away from the city center to the suburbs in virtually all industries. As the U.S. population also continues to suburbanize, larger proportions of metropolitan area employment and population are locating beyond the traditional central business districts along the nation's suburban beltways and the more distant fringes.

Job Sprawl and Poverty

For city residents whose low incomes restrict their housing choices, job decentralization may make it more difficult to find and maintain employment.

Understanding the association between employment decentralization and the suburbanization of poverty is important because of the continued growth of the suburban poor. In 2005, the suburban poor outnumbered their city counterparts by almost one million. And during the first year of the recession that began in 2007, suburbs added more than twice as many poor people as did their cities.

The suburban poor face unique disadvantages. These include concentration in inner-ring, disadvantaged, and jobs-poor suburbs; overreliance on public transportation, which often provides inferior access to and within suburban areas; and spatial mismatch between where the suburban poor live and the locations of important social services.

If the decentralization of employment increases the suburbanization of poverty, this may signal that the poor are able to move closer to labor market opportunities. Policies designed to facilitate this process, such as housing vouchers, may therefore produce direct and immediate results. But housing market segregation on the basis of race and class could limit mobility to suburbs, thereby limiting the poor's access to opportunity. For example, in 2000, poor blacks were considerably less suburbanized than poor Latinos or Asians. Moreover, low-income housing is much less available in suburbs than cities.

The Findings on Poverty Suburbanization

This report extends studies of poverty suburbanization by exploring one of its potential drivers, employment decentralization. It asks four key questions:

- Are the poor more or less suburbanized than the non-poor, and how does their location relate to employment decentralization in metropolitan areas?

- Does the relationship between poverty suburbanization and employment decentralization vary by race and ethnicity across different metropolitan areas?

- Do recent increases in the suburbanization of the poor relate to increases in employment decentralization?

- Do the suburban poor live in communities with similar levels of local employment opportunities as their non-poor counterparts? ...

These findings strongly suggest that employment decentralization is helping to drive the suburbanization of poverty.

Several results stand out. First, population and employment decentralization go hand-in-hand. At the metropolitan level, the degree of employment decentralization is strongly associated with the degree of suburbanization, although this relationship varies by demographic and economic group. Second, minorities and the poor are the least suburbanized, with poor blacks the least likely to reside in the suburbs. They also demonstrate the weakest association between suburbanization and employment decentralization. Third, changes in employment decentralization over time associate strongly with changes in suburbanization patterns. However, the poor appear considerably less likely to suburbanize in response to continued decentralization of employment (although the relationship is still positive). Finally, the poor are somewhat less likely to reside in jobs-rich suburbs, although the magnitude of this difference depends greatly on race and ethnicity and metro area characteristics.

Together, these findings strongly suggest that employment decentralization is helping to drive the suburbanization of poverty. However, the responsiveness of the poor to job sprawl is not as strong as it is for the population as a whole. Furthermore, when the poor reach the suburbs, they are more likely to live in jobs-poor areas that are frequently lower income and more disadvantaged—and potentially indistinguishable from disadvantaged central city areas. These patterns are sharpest for the black and Latino poor, and they are consistent with prior research documenting that racial and ethnic minorities have driven population growth in lower-income suburban areas characterized by weaker employment growth and lower access to good-paying jobs.

The Impact of Housing and Labor Market Policies

The demographic and economic disparities in the relationship between poverty suburbanization and job decentralization further suggest that frictions in housing markets limit the ability of the poor to follow jobs. These frictions may include the limited availability of affordable housing in jobs-rich, higher-income suburbs. This in turn may reflect zoning laws favoring single-family housing, the effect of development impact fees on affordable housing, and disproportionate location of low-income housing projects in central city or poor areas. At the same time, racial segregation in housing markets, including racial discrimination by banks in lending, by landlords or rental agents, or even resulting from racial preferences of residents, may drive these patterns as well. Moreover, zoning laws and development impact fees that limit low-income housing in suburban areas may themselves partly reflect racial preferences. Policies designed to minimize these frictions, such as providing more incentives for multifamily housing, reevaluating existing zoning laws and development impact fees, facilitating the use of housing vouchers in new suburban locations, and enforcing fair housing laws in suburban areas could go a long way toward easing mobility for the poor.

These findings raise a question, however. Are the poor hurt by their inability to readily follow jobs? Research would suggest yes, at least as measured by earnings and employment. These problems are compounded by low car ownership rates and limited information about distant job opportunities. Weaker informal networks, through which most lower-income workers seek jobs, limit their access to jobs outside their neighborhoods. For the poor in suburban areas, their access to homes in jobs-rich suburbs might be constrained by some combination of high housing costs, limited familiarity, and few social contacts in these areas. Moreover, the potentially higher commuting costs could be a disincentive to obtaining jobs in these areas. These costs are further compounded for those dependent on public transit because of sparse coverage of transit systems there.

These findings thus strongly suggest that housing and labor market policies should seek to maximize access to job opportunities for the poor, and low-income workers more broadly, throughout metropolitan areas, regardless of where the workers and the jobs are located.

Urban Sprawl Increases the Costs of Government-Subsidized Housing

Darby Minow Smith

Darby Minow Smith is assistant editor for Grist, *a nonprofit environmental news organization.*

Each year, U.S. taxpayers spend billions to subsidize affordable housing for low-income Americans. It's an important part of the social safety net we've built to keep families and the elderly from falling through the cracks. But there's a problem: A lot of that housing has been built far away from public transit, schools, and jobs. As a result, residents drive long distances, burning gobs of gas—and huge holes in their wallets—in the process.

For many residents of affordable housing, transportation and housing costs eat up over half of their income. For a struggling family, this can make healthy food, higher education, and health care seem as far-fetched as President Newt [Gingrich].

The Push to Reduce Transportation Costs

Lately, however, there's been a push to alleviate transportation costs for low-income families. Efforts on the state level show some promise, and officials at the federal level are expressing interest as well.

A growing number of forward-thinking state governments are already factoring in transportation costs when awarding tax breaks and funding for projects, giving preference to housing that is close to public transit. In the Chicago region, for example, 85 percent of the housing funded by the Illinois Housing Development Authority (IHDA) is now located within walking distance of bus or train stations.

Still, as a new study by the nonprofit Center for Neighborhood Technology (CNT) shows, policy changes like those in Illinois take time to have an effect. According to the study, the new policy favoring transit-friendly locales has yet to significantly reduce transportation costs for low-income residents, which range from $750 to $1,000 a month for a family making $3,445 a month, or 80 percent of the area median income.

We've been subsidizing sprawl for decades, and the recession has made jobs few and (literally) far between.

Part of the reason is that transit systems are not up to snuff. Living near a train station is great, but you're less apt to ride the train if it only passes through a couple times a day. Ditto with buses that don't get you where you need to go when you need to get there. In fact, during the study period, from 2001–2008, transit service to neighborhoods with IHDA-financed housing dropped 24 percent.

The Need for Dense Neighborhoods

But "it's not all about transit," says CNT's transportation and community development program director, María Choca Urban. In fact, of the key characteristics that correlate with low transportation costs, transit is the least important. More important than access to mass transit, are densely developed, compact neighborhoods with lots of amenities like grocery stores, schools, and jobs, Urban says—in other words, communities where residents don't have to travel long distances to meet their basic needs.

Jobs, you say? Dense neighborhoods? We've been subsidizing sprawl for decades, and the recession has made jobs few and (literally) far between. If Urban is right, and we're serious about building truly affordable housing, we've got our work cut out for us.

The slow progress on the state level has not deterred officials at the federal Department of Housing and Urban Development (HUD) from considering similar measures, however. HUD, which provides rental assistance for low-income families as well as grants and tax credits to affordable housing developments, is in the process of documenting transportation costs, neighborhood by neighborhood. HUD's model is loosely based on an index developed by CNT, which uses transportation costs to determine the "true affordability of housing based on its location."

The Importance of Information

Shelley Poticha, director of the Office of Sustainable Housing and Communities, says that policy changes like the one in Illinois are one possible tool. Another idea being floated is a labeling system much like what you would see if you were shopping for a new water heater. Instead of a sticker displaying energy costs, you would find information about the transportation costs associated with a house. Families receiving rental assistance could then compare different residences to find a location that fits within their budget.

"I think that consumers are really savvy and if we make this information available, easy to use, and free, then it seems like something the market will pick up," Poticha says. To illustrate her point, she references Walk Score, which a few years ago began ranking different areas of San Francisco on how many amenities were within walking distance. Within about a year, for sale signs in front of houses were listing their walk scores.

Poticha admits that remaking policy and changing tools is a difficult step that takes time, but she is optimistic about HUD's current direction. "What I'm seeing is phenomenal demand at the grassroots level," she says. Across the nation, people are "getting more and more vocal about the changes they want to see."

Helping low-income families make smarter location decisions and nudging affordable housing developers in the right direction would certainly help. But if the Chicago study is any indication, ditching the long car commute (via car, train, or otherwise) and creating walkable, tight-knit communities is the ultimate goal—and one that we won't achieve for a good, long while.

Downtown Urban Development Can Save Cities from Bankruptcy

Emily Badger

Emily Badger is a contributing writer to The Atlantic Cities. *Her work has appeared in* GOOD, The Christian Science Monitor, *and* The New York Times.

In the 1950s, the five-story brick Asheville Hotel in Asheville, North Carolina, started to fall into decline, presaging what would happen to most of the city's downtown over the next couple of decades. A department store moved into the ground floor while everything above it sat empty. Then the building got one of those ugly metal facades that's designed to distract from the fact that all the windows are boarded up. . . .

An Option for Broke Cities

Twenty years later, the local real-estate developer Public Interest Projects set its sights on the building for a mixed-use retail and residential property. Local bankers and businessmen said they were foolish. No one wants to live downtown, they said. And so no one was interested in financing the project. Public Interest Projects went ahead with its own money. . . .

"Usually people like to see these before-and-after pictures of buildings," says Joe Minicozzi, the new projects director at the firm who has now made something of a traveling road show with these photos. "And then we have the chaser of castor oil called economics."

Minicozzi at this point starts pulling out bar graphs and land-use maps and property-tax calculations, because he's not necessarily trying to make a point about the Asheville Hotel as much as he is about the fundamental math problem posed by modern cities in America.

In its vacant state in the 1970s, the Asheville Hotel didn't contribute much to the public coffers. Today, though, that same parcel of land is responsible for exponentially more property tax revenue that helps pay for police, parks and city streets.

We tend to think that broke cities have two options: raise taxes, or cut services. Minicozzi, though, is trying to point to the basic but long-buried math of our tax system that cities should be exploiting instead: Per-acre, our downtowns have the potential to generate so much more public wealth than low-density subdivisions or massive malls by the highway. And for all that revenue they bring in, downtowns cost considerably less to maintain in public services and infrastructure.

The really interesting math . . . comes not when we compare derelict buildings to their refurbished selves, but when we look at unsung half-block offices alongside what we think *are our big municipal money-makers: vast hotels, malls, big-box stores.*

Fixing Underutilized Buildings

"We really are kind of preachy, because we know it works," says Minicozzi, who has performed similar tax studies in 15 cities across the country. "And the reason we know it works is because cities have been here forever. That's all we're saying: think urban. When I talk with people about urbanism, we as hairless apes have lived in these things called cities for thousands of years. Now over these last 40 years, we think we don't need them any more?"

So, broke cities: Need money? If you've got underutilized buildings in your downtown, do anything you can to fix them up, because that's where your wealth comes from. This is Minicozzi's first lesson. . . .

An old JCPenney in downtown Asheville, sat vacant for 40 years before Minicozzi's firm bought and remodeled it.

It's now home to a beauty salon in the basement, retail on the ground floor, offices on the second floor and 19 condos above. In 1991, the taxable value of this vacant building was just $300,000. Now, this property that sits on one-fifth of an acre is worth $11 million.

Taxes by the Acre

The really interesting math, though, comes not when we compare derelict buildings to their refurbished selves, but when we look at unsung half-block offices alongside what we *think* are our big municipal money-makers: vast hotels, malls, big-box stores.

Asheville has a Super Walmart about two-and-a-half miles east of downtown. Its tax value is a whopping $20 million. But it sits on 34 acres of land. This means that the Super Walmart yields about $6,500 an acre in property taxes, while that remodeled JCPenney downtown is worth $634,000 in tax revenue per acre. (Add sales tax revenue, and the downtown property is still worth more than six times as much as the Walmart per acre.)

This is the cognitive blinder we bring to the economics of land use: We tend to compare buildings to each other, without looking at their unit value. This would be like comparing the fuel economy of the tank of a Ford F-150 to the tank of a Prius. We don't shop for vehicles that way, because that makes no sense. We look at miles-per-gallon, not miles-per-tank, because tanks come in all different sizes. We should look at buildings, Minicozzi argues, the exact same way.

"As a community, if you have a finite limit of land, would you want $6,500 or $20,000, or $634,000 downtown an acre?" he asks. "I tell people, 'What would you rather grow: wheat, soybeans or marijuana?' People understand that cash-crop concept, so why aren't we doing that downtown?"

This concept is true everywhere. In Raleigh, for instance, it would take 600 single-family homes on a 150-acre subdivision to equal the tax base of the 30-story Wells Fargo Capitol Center downtown. And it sits on 1.2 acres of land.

The Cost of Low-Density Development

All of this is also just looking at the revenue side of the ledger. Low-density development isn't just a poor way to make property-tax revenue. It's extremely expensive to maintain. In fact, it's only feasible if we're expanding development at the periphery into eternity, forever bringing in revenue from new construction that can help pay for the existing subdivisions we've already built.

Cities could generate wealth not by raising taxes, but by better exploiting the economics of land use.

Minicozzi made some of these calculations in a study of Sarasota, Florida. A downtown 357-unit multi-family complex on a 3.4-acre site there, he found, pays off its infrastructure in three years. A suburban subdivision on a 30-acre site will take 42 years to pay off. After two decades, that downtown multi-family complex will have made the city $33 million in net revenue. The suburban subdivision will still be $5 million in the hole.

"The thing is it all works fine when you have all this new growth and the new gap is met by all these new permit fees— that's like free money," Minicozzi says. "But if you and I go out and just keep eating McDonald's french fries, we're going to feel full, but is it providing enough sustenance for us?"

Cities everywhere are experiencing the collapse of that model now. But not many have caught on yet to the solution Minicozzi is talking about. If we look at the per-acre value of our land, and where that land is most valuable, cities could generate wealth not by raising taxes, but by better exploiting the economics of land use.

Downtown Asheville has been a windfall for the city since developers began reinvesting there, starting with the Asheville Hotel. . . . The taxable value of the property there has swelled in just 20 years.

The whole idea is pretty simple. But it's sort of baffling that we haven't been looking at our land this way for years. Cities, Minicozzi laments, are woefully ignorant about exactly which types of neighborhoods and development put the most financial strain on public coffers and which kick in the most money. This is why Minicozzi has been deploying every metaphor he can think of—cash crops, gas tanks, french fries—to beat home the math. . . .

To get back on sound financial footing, cities ought to start looking at all their land this way.

CHAPTER 4

How Should Urban Sprawl Be Managed?

Overview: Attempts at Managing Sprawl

T.A. Frank

T.A. Frank is a writer and editor at Washington Monthly *magazine.*

When developers unveiled the Solair, a 22-story luxury condominium designed for the Koreatown neighborhood of Los Angeles, even the mayor showed up for the ribbon cutting. Located above a subway stop at Wilshire Boulevard and Western Avenue, the Solair was supposed to embody the future of Los Angeles as a city focused on walking and mass transit. "Solair Wilshire is the perfect example of my vision for creating a transit-oriented city that brings business and housing to Los Angeles," Mayor Antonio Villaraigosa said.

That was in May 2009. Nearly two years later, few windows in the Solair are lit up at night. The national real-estate crash had long since caused speculators to flee the housing market, leaving behind only serious buyers who actually intend to live in their properties—except, apparently, in the Solair. While the median price for home sales in Los Angeles County has inched up since the Solair opened—from $247,000 in April 2009 to $270,000 in January 2011—the building has lowered its asking prices by more than a third, and they're still falling. Many other condominiums in downtown Los Angeles are having just as much trouble finding purchasers.

Did potential buyers of the Solair's apartments flee to distant, sprawling suburbs instead? Hardly. Those suburbs are in equally bad shape. On the outer rim of Corona, a city of about 125,000 southeast of L.A. in Riverside County, declines in prices have been among the steepest in the state. Corona's newest housing developments, built among outlying cow pastures, are made up of luxurious four-bedroom and five-bedroom stucco houses with swimming pools, hot tubs, and expansive lawns. But the residents talk about neighborhood deterioration and increases in crime. In Lancaster, a city in northern Los Angeles County, scores of homes that were built six years ago and purchased by middle-class commuters are now occupied by low-income renters using federal subsidies, while other houses stand empty. Gunfire often erupts after sunset.

So what do Southern California homebuyers want? To judge by the places where price declines are least severe, upper-middle-class buyers have flocked to established neighborhoods or cities with modest, but attractive, older houses, typically with three bedrooms and two baths. Much of Beverly Hills has housing like this. So does the Miracle Mile, a neighborhood a few miles west of the Solair. Given more choices, buyers want single-family homes that are not in sprawling suburbs. They want to live close to town centers but not in dense high-rises. In short, they want to live in the year 1925.

All urban planning rests on assumptions or guesses about people's preferences, and those are often wrong.

The trouble is, we're approaching 2025. By then, California is expected to add 7 million to 11 million people, about a quarter of its current population. (By 2050, the U.S. population is projected to reach 400 million, a 30 percent increase.) These new people will need homes, which can't all be three-bedroom bungalows close to downtown. They'll also need transportation. Automobile traffic and air pollution—already bad—stand to get worse.

The environmental costs of a sprawling population explain why the Democratic-run California Legislature passed Senate Bill 375 in 2008 with the goal of encouraging county governments to grow up rather than out. The legislation, signed into law by then-Gov. Arnold Schwarzenegger, empowers the state's Air Resources Board to set targets for emissions of pollutants, requires local governments to look for ways to handle a growing population without taking up more space, and gives first dibs on state transportation funds to locales devoted to mass transit.

Given the choices that California faced—permissive neglect or controlled development—legislators argued that the anti-sprawl law was the most sensible approach to managing air pollution, traffic congestion, and the loss of open spaces. Tall buildings such as the Solair usually put people within easy walking distance of stores and restaurants, without any need for new roads. The more they ride mass transit, the less they'll drive cars.

Environmentalists and planning experts around the world are paying attention to California's experiment in shaping housing patterns and urban growth. They see in the state's big cities the same problems that other metropolises face: clogged roads; strained water supplies; and, above all, excessive carbon emissions. If a state famed for its urban sprawl can change its ways, other places can, too. And if the problems can be solved without reducing the overall quality of life—that is, without making everyone miserable—then California could become an inspiring model.

Will the experiment succeed? Nobody knows yet. In theory, the California law will bring big changes. But all urban planning rests on assumptions or guesses about people's preferences, and those are often wrong.

The Pitfalls

Any serious attempt to judge the anti-sprawl law's success must wait at least a decade, possibly much longer. Still, some urban planners see promising indications of an improved approach to planning throughout the state.

"I don't want to be a Pollyanna about this, but so far I'm very impressed," said Marlon Boarnet, a University of California (Irvine) professor of planning, design, and economics who, for the Air Resources Board, has pored over two years of data in assessing the law's impact. Notably, he said, county governments have stepped back and—for a change—thought seriously about planning. Even city governments, often resistant to regional planning, have acted in good faith.

One thing the law has in its favor is that, despite the customary fear that regulation stifles economic growth, it might prove a boon for business. A study by University of California (Berkeley) urban planners Karen Chapple and Carrie Makarewicz found that most business growth in California during the past 15 years has been in locations with major infrastructure—roads, sewers, and such—already in place. Construction on cities' peripheries has been far less common. That's because typical business owners, like other people, enjoy working near residences, stores, and restaurants. A modicum of density allows a worker to walk to a Starbucks during lunch or stop at a CVS for mint-flavored floss. "By encouraging infill development"—building on land that's already developed— the anti-sprawl law "could very well help, not hinder, California's economic growth," Chapple and Makarewicz concluded.

Even when density is pursued for the most high-minded of reasons, after a while it offers diminishing returns, especially in reducing the use of cars.

There are reasons aplenty, however, for skepticism about visions of a denser—and happier—future for the state that pioneered urban sprawl. For one thing, implementation is everything. In many cities, especially in Los Angeles, the ideal of "walkability" and mass transit has been invoked to justify intrusive and ugly projects that real-estate developers and other urban power brokers champion.

Cary Brazeman, the owner of a marketing agency, became an unlikely crusader for urban livability in 2009, when developers tried to build a hulking condominium in his neighborhood on the west side of Los Angeles. "It was going to displace more tenants living under rent control than it was going to add affordable units," he said in an interview. "It didn't make sense in our neighborhood, and the rules of the game were being changed without due process." Since then, Brazeman has fought similarly high-handed planning all over the city.

Even when density is pursued for the most high-minded of reasons, after a while it offers diminishing returns, especially in reducing the use of cars. Kaid Benfield, a director at the Natural Resources Defense Council in Washington, has pointed to studies showing that an increase in density per acre from one household to 10 will reduce the use of automobiles by half. But doubling the density again, to 20 households per acre, will bring an additional auto cutback of only a fifth, with even scantier reductions from there. This is important because many of the world's biggest cities, including U.S. ones, already have a higher density than 10 households per acre.

Further complicating the prospect for density in housing to supplant—or complement—urban sprawl is that many cities in the American West are fairly new and poorly laid out for rail transit. By comparison, New York and Boston, with elaborate subway networks, were developed before the automobile was invented. But in other cities, especially in California, nearly all of the population growth and construction occurred while cars were already king. "We're having to figure out how to go in and retrofit those cities to accommodate higher density levels," UC professor Boarnet said.

Contrast that with the geography of growth experienced in Northern Virginia, which has seen extensive development along the subway lines that lead into Washington. Because the subway preceded the density, the town houses and condominiums along its route were built to take advantage of the Washington Metrorail system.

What Americans Want

There's another obstacle to encouraging denser development: Americans' love affair with their cars. Even if auto-dependent cities successfully bring mass transit within reach of more inhabitants, Americans don't necessarily want what they're supposed to want. In a 2002 opinion poll conducted by the Public Policy Institute of California, only 31 percent of Californians said they'd like to live in a neighborhood with dense development and mass transit. Even in the San Francisco Bay Area, where the living is dense and public transportation is extensive, 57 percent of respondents said they preferred a low-density, car-dependent lifestyle.

California's new density measure also leaves municipal parking policies untouched. When your rent includes a parking spot or two, as is customary in Los Angeles, then you're far more likely to fill that spot with a car, as University of California (Los Angeles) urban planner Donald C. Shoup notes in his book *The High Cost of Free Parking*. In fact, the zoning laws in many U.S. cities mandate that any new construction of office or residential space includes a minimum number of parking spaces—"like a fertility drug for cars," Shoup writes.

Around the world, people love their cars. As University of Southern California economist Peter Gordon pointed out, suburbanization is an international phenomenon. "People everywhere want autos, and when they get them, they enjoy vastly improved range and mobility," he said. "Trying to pin all this on U.S. policies, as many do, is silly. Have you been abroad lately?"

In fact, some Californians are so committed to holding on to their lifestyle that they've tried to sidestep the sprawl-or-density debate by simply freezing their communities in time. This is why a few cities have enacted slow-growth—or almost no-growth—policies. During the 1970s, for instance, the voters of Santa Barbara, a wealthy coastal town in Southern California, decided that the city population should cap out at 85,000. (It has crept up to 92,000.) For those who can afford to live there—increasingly, millionaires—Santa Barbara is still a dream of low-density, car-dependent living. A homeowner atop the hills of the Riviera neighborhood can hop in a car and be downtown on State Street, the main drag, in just a few minutes.

Suburbs have mushroomed because of middle-class residents fleeing bad schools and rising crime.

But slow-growth policies along with rapid population gains are bound to jack up the cost of living, as more and more people covet a limited supply of housing. Not surprisingly, Santa Barbara's inhabitants have increasingly become rich and elderly, and people who work there must often commute great distances from more-affordable places with less-restrictive growth policies. If all of California adopted slow-growth measures such as Santa Barbara's, the city's traffic might improve, but the children of today's Californians would wind up priced out of their native state and forced to move away. California has always been the place that people moved to.

Ultimately, however, the question of whether Americans would rather sprawl or bunch up may prove to be a distraction. Many buyers care less about a lawn versus an apartment balcony than about safety and schools. Neighborhoods with low crime rates and outstanding schools command high home prices, regardless of their density. Suburbs have mushroomed because of middle-class residents fleeing bad schools and rising crime. A neighborhood that offers safety and quality schools could well succeed in luring families into high-rises that lack parking.

Fixing urban schools is no simple matter, of course. But the crime problem is improving. In Los Angeles, the homicide rate has fallen to levels not seen since 1967, thanks mainly to a revamped police department. This in itself has attracted more middle-class homebuyers to the city, much as New York City experienced in the 1990s. Higher incomes, in turn, usually help to improve schools. All of which would bode well for California's experiment in fighting urban sprawl—and for the Solair.

Big Burdens from Growth Management

Randal O'Toole

Randal O'Toole is a senior fellow at the Cato Institute working on urban growth, public land, and transportation issues and author of The Best-Laid Plans: How Government Planning Harms Your Quality of Life, Your Pocketbook, and Your Future.

Median family incomes in Raleigh, N.C., almost are identical to those in Seattle, Wash., but a family purchasing a house in Seattle would have to pay more than twice as much as for a similar home in Raleigh. The additional cost almost entirely is due to a form of restrictive land-use regulation known as growth-management planning. As practiced in about a dozen states and a number of other urban regions, growth management puts the American dream of homeownership out of reach for many young and low-income families and was a major cause of the housing bubble that helped plunge the nation into recession.

The additional cost of housing in regions that use growth management can be called the planning tax. In many parts of the country, this tax averages hundreds of thousands of dollars per home. Growth management attempts to control either the rate of a city's or region's population growth or the location of that growth. Either way, it limits the ability of homebuilders to meet the demand for new housing. Thanks to growth management, someone buying a four-bedroom, two-and-one-half bath home would have to spend more than $1,100,000 in San Jose, Calif., which has practiced growth management since 1970, and more than $550,000 in Seattle, which has practiced growth management since 1985. That same house would cost less than $250,000 in Raleigh and other cities that have no growth management, such as Houston (Tex.), Kansas City (Mo.), and Louisville (Ky.).

The most popular form of growth management today is called smart growth, which uses urban-growth boundaries and other tools to restrict development beyond the urban fringe and instead promote high-density development in the cities. Such restrictions drive up land prices and particularly increase the cost of the type of housing that most people prefer: single-family homes with a yard. When new home prices rise, the cost of existing homes follow as homesellers see that other homes are getting more expensive. This means that any policy that makes new homes more expensive—whether it is growth boundaries, impact fees, or a lengthy permitting process—will make all housing less affordable.

Growth management is responsible for much of the recent subprime mortgage crisis.

Although American cities have been planning and zoning since before 1920, growth management only began in the 1960s, when a few cities and states adopted policies aimed at restricting the rate of growth or controlling where growth would take place. Boulder, Colo., for instance, limits the number of building permits that can be issued each year and purchases land outside the city limits to prevent developers from building at the urban fringe. In 1961, Hawaii passed a statewide growth-management law requiring all cities to write such plans. Oregon followed in 1973. California passed a law in 1963 that gave cities control over the rural areas in each county; this unintentionally became the state's growth-management act.

The most telling fact about the recent housing bubble is that it did not occur everywhere. As economist Paul Krugman notes, prices rose most in what he calls "the zoned zone," regions where land-use restrictions "made it hard to build new houses." In the rest of the country, prices rose not much faster than the rate of inflation. In fact, all but one of the states that saw rapid home price increases have state growth-management laws or local government restrictions on housing supply. The one exception, Nevada, is 90% owned by the Federal government. Prior to 2000, the state's growth was enabled by Federal land sales but, when such sales slowed, homebuilders in Las Vegas and Reno literally ran out of private land. So Nevada's growth management effectively resulted from Federal—rather than state or local—policies.

At the same time, all but one of the states that have passed growth-management laws saw housing prices increase rapidly after 2000. The one exception, Tennessee, passed its law in 1998, and the law's implementation has yet to restrict new home construction.

Growth management is responsible for much of the recent subprime mortgage crisis. Because state and local restrictions on housing supplies sent prices soaring, families who ordinarily would have qualified for prime loans were compelled to borrow at subprime rates. When the housing bubble burst, housing prices dropped, leaving many families with mortgages greater than the value of their house. The resulting credit crisis has shaken the American economy to its core.

This was not the first housing bubble the U.S. has experienced, but it was the first to affect so many homes. A bubble took place in the 1970s in just the few states that then had growth-management laws. After more regions wrote growth-management plans, a second bubble in the 1980s affected several more states. The most recent bubble covered about 40% of the nation's housing.

There is a strong correlation between the year states and regions write growth-management plans and the year, usually very shortly afterwards, when housing prices begin to rise sharply. Historically, U.S. housing prices have risen at about the rate of inflation but, when regions or cities write growth-management plans, prices suddenly accelerate and housing quickly becomes unaffordable.

Research by Harvard University economist Edward Glaeser has found that land-use restrictions not only increase housing prices, they makes those prices more volatile. "If an area has a $10,000 increase in housing prices during one period, relative to national and regional trends," says Glaeser, "that area will lose $3,300 in housing value over the next five-year period."

The planning taxes paid by buyers of new homes simply are absorbed by the higher costs of home construction.

Note that prices never fall to their original levels. This means that home prices in places like California, which has seen three booms and busts since 1970, become more unaffordable with each new boom. Of course, prices are higher in California partly because California incomes are higher than in many other states. A more valid measure of housing affordability is median home price divided by median family income, known as the price-to-income ratio. If the price-to-income ratio is less than 3.0, a median family can pay off a six percent mortgage on a median home out of 30% of its income in less than 15 years. At a ratio of 5, the family would have to spend 36% of its income to pay off the loan in 30 years. Since prime loans generally limit mortgage payments to about 30% of income, high price-to-income ratios force more families to get subprime mortgages.

Not surprisingly, the states with the highest price-to-income ratios are those with growth-management laws, such as Hawaii and California. The average price-to-income ratio in California is more than 8 and, in some of the state's urban areas, it is more than 10. By contrast, the price-to-income ratios in several fast-growing states with no growth-management laws, including North Carolina and Texas, are 2.5 or less.

Nationally, people who bought homes in 2006 were socked with more than $250,000,000,000 in planning taxes. About half of this was in California. Most of the rest was in nine states with mandatory growth-management laws—Arizona, Florida, Hawaii, Maryland, New Jersey, Oregon, Rhode Island, Vermont, and Washington—or in urban areas such as Denver (Colo.) and the Twin Cities (Minn.) that have adopted regional growth-management plans without state mandates. It is not clear that homebuyers are getting anything for this tax. Planners say the goal of growth management is to make cities more livable, but is there anything planners have done to make, say, San Jose (Calif.) more livable than Dallas (Tex.)? If the benefits are murky, it certainly is clear that planners have made San Jose, where the price-to-income ratio is more than 9, far less affordable than Dallas, where it only is slightly more than 2. No wonder that, since 1990, the Dallas urbanized area has grown by 40%, while Silicon Valley, the heart of the nation's fastest-growing industries, has grown by 10%.

The planning taxes paid by buyers of new homes simply are absorbed by the higher costs of home construction. Other than the impact fees collected by local governments, they mostly are a dead-weight loss to society.

The planning taxes paid by buyers of existing homes at least have the virtue of not being a total loss, as they become windfall profits for the homesellers. Yet, homeowners may find that the benefits they get from growth management partly are an illusion. While they can borrow against their increased equity, they run a greater risk of seeing prices decline and owing more than their homes are worth. The only way they truly can realize their gains from high housing prices is to sell and move to an area that has not adopted such strict land-use policies.

Homeowners in high-priced markets who want to move to a larger house in the same region face the same cost barriers as first-time homebuyers. The worst cases are when—perhaps due to job transfers after a housing bubble has burst—people have to sell their homes "short," that is, for less than the amount remaining on their mortgages. Even if some home-owners profit nicely from growth management, this raises an-other issue: people who already own their own homes tend to have higher incomes and be wealthier than first-time home-buyers. So, the planning tax is a reverse-Robin Hood program: taking from the poor and giving to the rich.

A study by an Oregon economist, Randall Pozdena, found that, if all states had adopted his state's smart-growth policies before 1990, more than 1,000,000 families that had become homeowners since 1990 would not have been able to purchase their homes. At least one-quarter of those families would be minorities, leading Joseph Perkins, a black radio and newspa-per commentator in the San Francisco Bay area, to observe, "Smart growth is the new Jim Crow."

Studies show that owner-occupied homes create more stable neighborhoods, provide a better environment for raising children, and are a generator of wealth.

Nationally, more than 72% of white families own their own homes, but only 46% of black and Hispanic families are homeowners. High housing prices actually are driving black families out of the San Francisco Bay area. Intentionally or not, smart growth has become just one more impediment to families trying to escape poverty.

To make up for the loss in housing affordability, many ar-eas that have passed growth-management plans have followed with rules requiring homebuilders to sell or rent a certain per-centage of their homes to low- or moderate-income families at below-market prices. However, research by economists at

San Jose State University has proven that this is self-defeating because homebuilders merely pass the costs onto other home-buyers, thus making the overall housing market even less affordable than before.

From 1940–60, U.S. homeownership rates grew from 44% to 62%. Since 1960, they have grown a mere seven percent. Many other countries, including Ireland, Italy, and Spain, enjoy much higher homeownership rates. Growth management is a major reason for the slowdown. Homeownership in California and Oregon peaked in 1960, while it has continued to grow in most states with no growth-management laws. Without growth management, overall U.S. rates would be well above 70%.

Why is homeownership so important? Studies show that owner-occupied homes create more stable neighborhoods, provide a better environment for raising children, and are a generator of wealth. Homeowners tend to take better care of their dwellings than renters. This means people who own their own homes usually live better than those who rent, and neighborhoods dominated by owner-occupied homes more likely are nicer than those dominated by renter-occupied homes. This especially is important for families with children. After adjusting for the income and education of their parents, children in families who own their own homes do better in school than those in families who rent—and the difference is greatest in low-income families.

Peruvian economist Hernando de Soto attributes the wealth of the U.S. in part to the ease with which people can buy their homes and then leverage the equity to start small businesses. "The single most important source of funds for new businesses in the United States is a mortgage on the entrepreneur's house," de Soto stresses.

Some people think homeownership has a downside. A study in Britain found that homeownership actually is an impediment to finding a job—but this, too, is due to growth management. Britain has practiced growth management since 1947, and price-to-income ratios there are between 6 and 9. British neighborhoods with high homeownership rates, the study found, also had high unemployment rates. When housing costs are so high, people cannot afford the realtor fees to sell their homes, so they remain jobless rather than move to a place where they can find work.

Surveys show that more than 80% of Americans would rather live in a single-family home with a yard than live closer to shops, jobs, and transit.

So far, this is not widespread in the U.S., where states and regions that do not practice growth management act as relief valves for the ones that do. However, "places with rapid price increases over one five-year period are more likely to have income and employment declines over the next five-year period," Glaeser notes.

Politically, the key to keeping housing affordable is to make sure that homebuilders have access to developable land outside of city limits. So long as this remains true, cities will welcome development within their boundaries to avoid losing property and sales tax revenues. If, however, cities can restrict development in rural areas, as they can under California's 1963 law, then they will feel free to impose high impact fees, add red tape to the permitting process, and otherwise increase the cost of home construction within their boundaries.

Promoting Compact Cities

Smart growth explicitly seeks to give cities such control over rural development in order to promote more compact cities. Planners say this is needed to limit urban "sprawl," a pejorative term for the way most Americans live: in single-family homes with large yards. Moreover, this is the way most people say they aspire to live. Surveys show that more than 80% of

Americans would rather live in a single-family home with a yard than live closer to shops, jobs, and transit. Moreover, this is not an exclusive American preference, as European cities also have suburbanized, and their suburbs, indicates urban historian Peter Hall, are "almost indistinguishable" from those in the U.S.

It is easy for people who already own their own homes to imagine that all future residents of their cities or regions will be happy to live in condos or apartments, but this is why growth management leads to unaffordable housing. Most people are not happy living in high densities, so the price of single-family homes goes up.

Contrary to some claims, there is no evidence that sprawl causes obesity or other health problems. Although research shows that people who are obese are slightly more inclined to live in the suburbs than others, the suburbs are not responsible for their health problems—nor do we need to curb sprawl to protect the environment. As Robert Bruegmann, author of *Sprawl: A Compact History*, points out, "The environmental effects of sprawl are benign."

Despite the impression you might get if you drive exclusively on Interstate freeways, urban growth does not threaten our farms, forests, or open spaces. The Census Bureau says that all U.S. urban areas occupy less than three percent of the nation's land. You might think that, as the nation's most populous state, California is overrun with sprawl. In fact, the state's growth-management plans have jammed 95% of its residents into just 5.1% of the state's land, making California urban areas the second most dense in the nation (trailing only New York City). If California residents had been allowed to "sprawl" at the same densities as other urban areas, they would occupy 8.5% of the state. Even the most ardent lovers of open space should find it hard to argue that tripling the state's housing costs is a fair price to pay for saving a mere 3.4% of the state's rural open space.

In most other states with growth-management laws, the amount of open space those laws protect is even more insignificant. Oregon's 1973 law restrains most development to within urban-growth boundaries that cover just 1.25% of the state. Yet, if Oregon's urban densities were the same as those in the rest of the nation, the additional sprawl would cover merely one-third of a percent more of the state's land.

Efforts to control sprawl have led to very real difficulties: unaffordable housing, higher land costs for business and industry, housing bubbles and busts, and increasing barriers to homeownership for low- and moderate-income families.

Of course, when we say a particular law has "protected" open space from development, we usually mean that the law has denied rural landowners the right to use their property as they see fit. Because landowners receive no compensation for this taking of their property rights, it should be viewed with even greater outrage than the Supreme Court's recent decision allowing cities to take people's land by eminent domain—with compensation—and give that land to private developers.

Zoning originally was created to protect residential neighborhoods from the pollution of industry or the traffic generated by shopping malls. However, it is one thing to say, "You can build a house next to my house but not a factory because the factory will make me and my neighbors sick." It is quite another to say, "You can't develop your land at all just because I like the idea that every rural acre stays rural forever."

Russians say that Americans do not have any real problems, so they have to make them up. Urban sprawl is one of those made-up problems. Unfortunately for U.S. citizens, efforts to control sprawl have led to very real difficulties: unaffordable housing, higher land costs for business and industry, housing bubbles and busts, and increasing barriers to home-ownership for low- and moderate-income families.

States that have passed growth-management laws should repeal them. States that have not passed such laws should avoid them—only then will we see homeownership rates rise and more individuals achieve the American dream of owning the home of their choice.

To Rethink Sprawl, Start with Offices

Louise A. Mozingo

Louise A. Mozingo is professor in the Department of Landscape Architecture and Environmental Planning at the University of California, Berkeley, and author of Pastoral Capitalism: A History of Suburban Corporate Landscapes.

In an era of concern about climate change, residential suburbs are the focus of a new round of critiques, as low-density developments use more energy, water and other resources. But so far there's been little discussion of that other archetype of sprawl, the suburban office.

The Suburban Office

Rethinking sprawl might begin much more effectively with these business enclaves. They cover vast areas and are occupied by a few powerful entities, corporations, which at some point will begin spending their ample reserves to upgrade, expand or replace their facilities.

The bucolic business office is not a state-of-the-art workplace but rather a decades-old model of corporate retreat. In 1942 the AT&T Bell Telephone Laboratories moved from its offices in Lower Manhattan to a new, custom-designed facility on 213 acres outside Summit, N.J.

The location provided space for laboratories and quiet for acoustical research, and new features: parking lots that allowed scientists and engineers to drive from their nearby suburban homes, a spacious cafeteria and lounge and, most surprisingly, views from every window of a carefully tended pastoral landscape designed by the Olmsted brothers, sons of the designer of Central Park.

Corporate management never saw the city center in the same way again. Bell Labs initiated a tide of migration of white-collar workers, especially as state and federal governments conveniently extended highways into the rural edge.

A Form of Segregation

In metropolitan areas across America, corporate campuses for research and development units proliferated and top executives ensconced themselves in palatial estates like the Deere & Co. Administrative Center outside Moline, Ill. Meanwhile, branch offices, small corporations and start-ups found footing in the office parks that lined suburban highways and arterial roads, like those of Silicon Valley in California and the Research Triangle Park in North Carolina.

Born in an era of seemingly limitless resources, this pastoral capitalism restructured the landscape of metropolitan regions; today it accounts for well over half the office space in the United States.

Rethinking pastoral capitalism is integral to creating a connected, compact metropolitan landscape that tackles rather than sidesteps a post-peak-oil future.

Yet suburban offices are even more unsustainably designed than residential suburbs. Sidewalks extend only between office buildings and parking lots, expanses of open space remain private and the spreading of offices over large zones precludes effective mass transit.

These workplaces embody a new form of segregation, where civic space connecting work to the shops, housing, recreation and transportation that cities used to provide is entirely absent. Corporations have cut themselves off from participation in a larger public realm.

Three Steps Toward Sustainability

Rethinking pastoral capitalism is integral to creating a connected, compact metropolitan landscape that tackles rather than sidesteps a post-peak-oil future. This requires three interrelated strategies. State and federal governments should stop paying for new highway extensions that essentially subsidize the conversion of agricultural land for development, including corporate offices. Existing infrastructure needs maintenance and renewal, not expansion.

Suburban jurisdictions that now require little of the next corporate campus other than plentiful parking can demand more. For instance, they can use zoning codes to require pedestrian, bicycle and mass-transit links to adjacent residential developments. Add to the mix new public spaces, a greater diversity of uses, and transit between multiple employment centers and residential districts—not only to and from the downtown—and suburban corporate offices could initiate a wave of reform.

While suburban offices will continue to exist, some corporations can re-occupy city centers that they abandoned two generations ago. Development parcels, vacant offices and economic subsidies lie waiting in cities like Cleveland, Hartford, Raleigh, N.C., and Birmingham, Ala. These downtowns are well served by transit and pedestrian connections, a mix of retail and service uses, and a surprising amount of newly built and renovated housing where workers can live.

All three steps—a halt to agricultural land conversion, connecting dispersed employment centers with alternative transit, and encouraging downtown development—are needed to create renewed, civic-minded corporate workplaces and, in the process, move toward sustainable cities. Even leaving aside climate change, very soon the price of energy will make the dispersed, unconnected, low-density city-building pattern impossibly costly. Those jurisdictions and businesses that first create livable, workable, post-peak-oil metropolitan regions are the ones that will win the future.

Government Should Not Discourage Suburban Development

Wendell Cox

Wendell Cox is head of Demographia, an international public policy and consulting firm, who specializes in urban policy, transportation, and demographics.

It's no secret that California's regulatory and tax climate is driving business investment to other states. California's high cost of living also is driving people away. Since 2000 more than 1.6 million people have fled, and my own research as well as that of others points to high housing prices as the principal factor.

The exodus is likely to accelerate. California has declared war on the most popular housing choice, the single family, detached home—all in the name of saving the planet.

Government Restrictions on New Housing

Metropolitan area governments are adopting plans that would require most new housing to be built at 20 or more to the acre, which is at least five times the traditional quarter acre per house. State and regional planners also seek to radically restructure urban areas, forcing much of the new hyperdensity development into narrowly confined corridors.

In San Francisco and San Jose, for example, the Association of Bay Area Governments has proposed that only 3% of new housing built by 2035 would be allowed on or beyond the "urban fringe"—where current housing ends and the countryside begins. Over two-thirds of the housing for the projected two million new residents in these metro areas would be multifamily—that is, apartments and condo complexes—and concentrated along major thoroughfares such as Telegraph Avenue in the East Bay and El Camino Real on the Peninsula.

For its part, the Southern California Association of Governments wants to require more than one-half of the new housing in Los Angeles County and five other Southern California counties to be concentrated in dense, so-called transit villages, with much of it at an even higher 30 or more units per acre.

The Impact of Restrictive Regulations

To understand how dramatic a change this would be, consider that if the planners have their way, 68% of new housing in Southern California by 2035 would be condos and apartment complexes. This contrasts with Census Bureau data showing that single-family, detached homes represented more than 80% of the increase in the region's housing stock between 2000 and 2010.

The love affair urban planners have for a future ruled by mass transit will be obscenely expensive and would not reduce traffic congestion.

The campaign against suburbia is the result of laws passed in 2006 (the Global Warming Solutions Act) to reduce greenhouse gas emissions and in 2008 (the Sustainable Communities and Climate Protection Act) on urban planning. The latter law, as the *Los Angeles Times* aptly characterized it, was intended to "control suburban sprawl, build homes closer to downtown and reduce commuter driving, thus decreasing climate-changing greenhouse gas emissions." In short, to discourage automobile use.

If the planners have their way, the state's famously unaffordable housing could become even more unaffordable.

Over the past 40 years, median house prices have doubled relative to household incomes in the Golden State. Why? In 1998, Dartmouth economist William Fischel found that California's housing had been nearly as affordable as the rest of the nation until the more restrictive regulations, such as development moratoria, urban growth boundaries, and overly expensive impact fees came into effect starting in the 1970s. Other economic studies, such as by Stephen Malpezzi at the University of Wisconsin, also have documented the strong relationship between more intense land-use regulations and exorbitant house prices.

The Government Preference for Transit

The love affair urban planners have for a future ruled by mass transit will be obscenely expensive and would not reduce traffic congestion. In San Diego, for example, an expanded bus and rail transit system is planned to receive more than half of the $48.4 billion in total highway and transit spending through 2050. Yet transit would increase its share of travel to a measly 4% from its current tiny 2%, according to data in the San Diego Association of Governments regional transportation plan. This slight increase in mass transit ridership would be swamped by higher traffic volumes.

Higher population densities in the future means greater traffic congestion, because additional households in the future will continue to use their cars for most trips. In the San Diego metropolitan area, where the average one-way work trip travel time is 28 minutes, only 14% of work and higher education locations could be reached within 30 minutes by transit in 2050. But 70% or more of such locations will continue to be accessible in 30 minutes by car.

Rather than protest the extravagance, California Attorney General Kamala D. Harris instead has sued San Diego because she thinks transit was not favored enough in the plan and thereby violates the legislative planning requirements enacted in 2006 and 2008. Her predecessor (Jerry Brown, who is now the governor) similarly sued San Bernardino County in 2007.

California's war on suburbia is unnecessary, even considering the state's lofty climate-change goals. For example, a 2007 report by McKinsey, co-sponsored by the Environmental Defense Fund and the Natural Resources Defense Council, concluded that substantial greenhouse gas emissions reductions could be achieved while "traveling the same mileage" and without denser urban housing. The report recommended cost-effective strategies such as improved vehicle economy, improving the carbon efficiency of residential and commercial buildings, upgrading coal-fired electricity plants, and converting more electricity production to natural gas.

Ali Modarres of the Edmund G. "Pat" Brown Institute of Public Affairs at California State University, Los Angeles has shown that a disproportionate share of migrating households are young. This is at least in part because it is better to raise children with backyards than on condominium balconies. A less affordable California, with less attractive housing, could disadvantage the state as much as its already destructive policies toward business.

Parking Needs to Be Restricted in Order to Limit Urban Sprawl

Katharine Mieszkowski

Katharine Mieszkowski is a senior reporter for The Bay Citizen *in Berkeley, California, covering the environment and health.*

In Tippecanoe County, Ind., there are 250,000 more parking spaces than registered cars and trucks. That means that if every driver left home at the same time and parked at the local mini-marts, grocery stores, churches and schools, there would still be a quarter of a million empty spaces. The county's parking lots take up more than 1,000 football fields, covering more than two square miles, and that's not counting the driveways of homes or parking spots on the street. In a community of 155,000, there are 11 parking spaces for every family.

The Paradox of Parking

Bryan Pijanowski, a professor of forestry and natural resources at Purdue University, which is located in Tippecanoe, documented the parking bounty in a study released this September. When it made the news, Pijanowski got puzzled reactions from locals. In short, they said: "Are you crazy? I can never find parking where I'm going!"

That's the paradox of parking. No matter how much land we pave for our idle cars, it always seems as if there isn't enough. That's America. We're all about speed and convenience. We don't want to walk more than two blocks, if that. So we remain wedded to our cars, responsible for "high CO_2

emissions, urban sprawl, increased congestion and gas usage, and even hypertension and obesity," says Amelie Davis, a Purdue graduate student who worked on the study.

Despite all the environmental evils blamed on the car and its enablers—General Motors, the Department of Transportation, Porsche, Robert Moses, suburban developers—parking has slipped under the radar. Yet much of America's urban sprawl, its geography of nowhere, stems from the need to provide places for our cars to chill. In the past few years, a host of forward-looking city planners have introduced plans to combat the parking scourge. This year, some are making real progress.

As parking lots proliferate, they decrease density and increase sprawl.

The Impact of Parking Requirements

Our story begins in the 1920s with the birth of a piece of esoteric regulation, the "minimum parking requirement." Before parking meters and residential parking permits, cities feared that they were running out of street parking. So municipalities began ordering businesses to provide parking and wrote zoning restrictions to ensure it. Columbus, Ohio, was first, requiring apartment buildings in 1923 to provide parking. In 1939, Fresno, Calif., decreed that hospitals and hotels must do the same. By the '50s, the parking trend exploded. In 1946, only 17 percent of cities had parking requirements. Five years later, 71 percent did.

Today, those regulations could fill a book, and do. The American Planning Association's compendium of regulations, "Parking Standards," numbers 181 pages. It lists the minimum parking requirements for everything from abattoirs to zoos. It is a city planner's bible.

To Donald Shoup, a professor of urban planning at UCLA, parking requirements are a bane of the country. "Parking requirements create great harm: they subsidize cars, distort transportation choices, warp urban form, increase housing costs, burden low income households, debase urban design, damage the economy, and degrade the environment," he writes in his book, *The High Cost of Free Parking*.

Americans don't object, because they aren't aware of the myriad costs of parking, which remain hidden. In large part, it's business owners, including commercial and residential landlords, who pay to provide parking places. They then pass on those costs to us in slightly higher prices for rent and every hamburger sold.

"Parking appears free because its cost is widely dispersed in slightly higher prices for everything else," explains Shoup. "Because we buy and use cars without thinking about the cost of parking, we congest traffic, waste fuel, and pollute the air more than we would if we each paid for our own parking. Everyone parks free at everyone else's expense, and we all enjoy our free parking, but our cars are choking our cities."

Parking Lots and Sprawl

It's a self-perpetuating cycle. As parking lots proliferate, they decrease density and increase sprawl. In 1961, when the city of Oakland, Calif., started requiring apartments to have one parking space per apartment, housing costs per apartment increased by 18 percent, and urban density declined by 30 percent. It's a pattern that's spread across the country.

In cities, the parking lots themselves are black holes in the urban fabric, making city streets less walkable. One landscape architect compares them to "cavities" in the cityscape. Downtown Albuquerque, N.M., now devotes more land to parking than all other land uses combined. Half of downtown Buffalo, N.Y., is devoted to parking. And one study of Olympia, Wash., found that parking and driveways occupied twice as much land as the buildings that they served.

Patrick Siegman, a transportation planner, who is a principal with Nelson\Nygaard Consulting Associates in San Francisco, says Americans are gradually waking up to the downside of parking requirements—at least in one way. "Americans love traditional American small towns, main streets and historic districts," he says. "But largely because of minimum parking requirements, it's completely illegal to build anything like that again in most American cities. It's really hard to build anything where anyone would want to walk from one building to the next."

The environmental impacts of all this parking go way beyond paving paradise.

Parking regulations vary locally, but a typical one in suburban communities requires four parking spaces for every 1,000 square feet of office space. Yet, typically, just over two spaces per 1,000 square feet are used. A classic restaurant parking regulation might require 20 parking spaces per 1,000 square feet of restaurant, which can mean more than five times the space for cars than for diners and chefs.

Wonder why the mall parking lot is half empty most of the time? Developers build parking lots to accommodate shoppers on the busiest shopping day of the year—the day after Thanksgiving—so that shoppers need never, ever park on the street. Similarly, the church parking lot is designed to accommodate Christmas and Easter services. So a whole lot of land gets paved over that doesn't have to be, transportation planners argue.

The Environmental Impact

The environmental impacts of all this parking go way beyond paving paradise. The impervious surfaces of parking lots accumulate pollutants, according to Bernie Engel, a professor of agricultural engineering at Purdue. Along with dust and dirt, heavy metals in the air like mercury, copper and lead settle onto the lots' surfaces in a process called dry deposition. These particles come from all kinds of diffuse sources, such as industry smokestacks, automobiles and even home gas water heaters.

"If they were naturally settling on a tree or grass, they would wash off those and into the soil, and the soil would hold them in place, so they wouldn't get into the local stream, lake or river," Engel says.

But when the same substances settle on parking lots, rain washes them into streams, lakes and rivers. Engel calculates that the Tippecanoe land used for parking creates 1,000 times the heavy-metal runoff that it would if used for agriculture. Because the surface of the lots doesn't absorb water, it also creates 25 times the water runoff that agricultural land would, which can increase erosion in local waterways.

There's a burgeoning movement among urban planners, transportation advocates and city officials to manage parking without blindly building more of it.

Parking lots also contribute to the "urban heat island effect." The steel, concrete and blacktops of buildings, roads and parking lots absorb solar heat during the day, making urban areas typically 2 to 5 degrees hotter than the surrounding countryside. "This is most apparent at nighttime, when the surrounding area is cooler, and the urban area starts radiating all this heat from the urban structures," explains Dev Niyogi, an assistant professor at Purdue, who is the Indiana state climatologist.

The urban heat island effect can be so dramatic that it changes the weather. One Indianapolis study found that thunderstorms that reach the city often split in two, going around it, and merging again into one storm after the urban area. "The urban heat island is not simply a temperature issue. It could affect our water availability," says Niyogi.

The Search for a Solution

In Tippecanoe, Pijanowski thinks the county could take steps to keep parking from eating up more land. With changes to zoning laws, a church and a school could share a parking lot, with the worshippers using it on the weekend, and the school kids and teachers parking in it during the week. "These new parking lots that are being built on the urban fringe are huge," says Pijanowski. "They're mega-lots that are servicing mega-buildings for big-box retailers and mega churches. Even our new schools in rural communities have huge parking lots. Having a parking space seems to be one of those amenities that you think is a good thing, but it probably isn't."

Still, there are few frustrations like driving around looking for a parking space, which has its own environmental impacts. Shoup studied a 15-block district in Los Angeles and found that drivers spent an average of 3.3 minutes looking for parking, driving about half a mile each. Over the course of a year, Shoup calculated the cruising in that small area would amount to 950,000 excess miles traveled, equal to 38 trips around the earth, wasting about 47,000 gallons of gas, and producing 730 tons of carbon dioxide that contribute to global warming.

But if simply requiring businesses to build more parking isn't the answer, what is? Today there's a burgeoning movement among urban planners, transportation advocates and city officials to manage parking without blindly building more of it.

Some cities, like Seattle and Petaluma, Calif., are loosening or chucking their minimum parking requirements. Great Britain found that minimum parking requirements bred such bad land-use policies that the nation recently outlawed them entirely. It's a policy that has appeal for both sides of the aisle.

"Liberals can love it because it does a huge amount on the affordability of housing, reducing traffic, improving the environment. And conservatives can love it because it's deregulation," says Siegman.

The Impact of Price

For his part, Shoup wants street parking to be priced at a market rate, so it can compete with lots and garages. Raising rates in the most congested areas will free up space curbside by inspiring thrifty drivers to park farther from their destinations, or—heaven forefend!—take the bus or train. To be politically feasible, he wants to see cities use the money raised by those increased fees to improve the city streets where they're collected, cleaning up graffiti or street cleaning, so shoppers and businesses can see the benefits of where that money is going.

Some cities are putting his theories to the test. In Redwood City, Calif., which boomed during the Gold rush by processing and shipping lumber to San Francisco, city planners are trying to revitalize the historic downtown by luring businesses and shoppers back from the far-flung malls and big-box stores. Yet adding parking spaces would mean adding parking garages, where capital costs can run $20,000 to $30,000 per parking space.

Recently, the city managed to subvert the parking code bible and add a 20-screen movie theater with 4,200 seats without adding more than a thousand parking spaces. Even before the cinema opened, on Friday and Saturday nights, drivers trying to go to restaurants and clubs circled the block searching for the elusive free street spaces, creating gridlock. Meanwhile, parking lots a few blocks away stood half empty. "We had plenty of parking," explains Dan Zack, downtown development coordinator for Redwood City. "What we had was a management problem, not a supply problem."

Transportation planners contend this is true in many urban areas, where street parking is free, and everyone is trying to grab a coveted space right in front of their destination. "You could add another 10,000 parking spaces to a place like downtown Redwood City, and it still wouldn't help you empty out the overfill on street spaces," says Siegman.

Ever since their first game of Monopoly, Americans have been conditioned to think that parking is free.

To prevent drivers from circling, Redwood City raised the prices of parking on the street from zero in the evening to 75 cents an hour on the main drag, and 50 cents and 25 cents in the surrounding streets until 8 p.m. Even farther from the center of the action, parking is still free on the street. Drivers searching for a good deal quickly caught on and went to the surrounding streets, cheaper parking lots and garages, which can be free with validation. Other cities, such as Ventura and Glendale, both in Southern California, are adopting similar schemes.

In Brooklyn, N.Y., transportation advocates are pushing for the city to consider doing the same. A survey by Transportation Alternatives, an advocacy group for bicyclists, walkers and public-transit users in New York City, found that 45 percent of drivers surveyed in Park Slope were just cruising looking for parking. And street parking was so overcrowded that one in six cars on the main drag, Seventh Avenue, was parked illegally. Only increases in the price of street parking can fix the problem, they contend.

"For the past 100 years, traffic engineers looked at problems like this, and said, 'Oh, the problem is that we don't have enough parking.' That's what got us into the nightmare that we have today," says Wiley Norvell, a spokesperson for Transportation Alternatives. "What we have to start doing is managing the demand for parking, and the way you manage demand is through pricing. The logic with parking for as long as anyone can remember has been supply-oriented. What that does is induce demand: The more roads you have, the more parking you have, the more cars you have." The hope is, of course, to create more incentive to bike, walk or take the bus, instead of driving.

But it's tough to convince drivers to accept that they might have to pay for something that they're used to thinking that they get for nothing, even if they're really paying for it in all kinds of invisible ways. Ever since their first game of Monopoly, Americans have been conditioned to think that parking is free. "I think that we've done things wrong for so long that it takes a while to break all our bad habits of wanting to be freeloaders," says Shoup. "We know that land is fabulously valuable and housing is expensive, but somehow we think we can park for free. We can't."

Government Should Not Coerce Housing and Transportation Choices

Ronald D. Utt

Ronald D. Utt is the Herbert and Joyce Morgan Senior Research Fellow at The Heritage Foundation.

President Barack Obama's early comments on his opposition to suburban sprawl and his intention to alter the way Americans live and travel took a step closer to reality when he created an interdepartmental initiative on housing and transportation costs. A March [2009] press release issued by the U.S. Department of Transportation (DOT) and the U.S. Department of Housing and Urban Development (HUD) announced a new interagency partnership to create "affordable, sustainable communities." Included among its many goals are projects to:

- Develop a new cost index that combines housing and transportation costs into a single measure to better illuminate the true costs by "redefining affordability and making it transparent,"

- Encourage "transportation choice," and

- Require even more planning by the many federally funded regional planning entities that are already attempting to guide Americans toward a supposedly better life.

Rich in the sort of progressive euphemisms used to mask real intentions, the press release heralds a process that could likely lead to an unprecedented federal effort to force Americans into an antiquated lifestyle that was common to the early years of the previous century. More specifically, these initiatives reflect an escalation in what is shaping up as President Obama's apparent intent to re-energize and lead the Left's longstanding war against America's suburbs.

The Liberals' Anti-Suburban Bias

Long ago, when it focused on the plight of low-income families, the American Left welcomed the suburbs as a healthy alternative to the airless tenements, congestion, and industrial concentration that characterized the cities and their working-class residents in the late 19th century. By the 1950s, however, it had become more fashionable for liberals to turn against the suburbs when a more prosperous America looked outside the central cities for better housing and public services and, in the process, abandoned public transportation for the flexibility, mobility, and privacy of automobiles.

Today, approximately 75 percent of Americans live in the suburbs, and only a handful of older cities that have not annexed suburban areas have populations exceeding their 1950 levels. Despite these near-universal preferences, however, many liberals continue to oppose the trend of suburbanization.

Despite the imposition of the many regulatory obstacles to buying homes in the suburbs ... the vast majority of American households opted to live in the suburbs instead of the more fashionable, albeit still dysfunctional, central cities or the older close-in suburbs.

Their efforts bore some fruit in the 1990s when the environmental movement joined forces with the anti-suburban Left to create the Smart Growth and New Urbanist movements. While both movements encouraged the concentration of people in denser communities that relied less on the automobile for transportation, both were quickly corrupted by the anti-growth, not-in-my-backyard (NIMBY) factions that used the rhetoric (and acquiescence) of the Left to adopt exclusionary laws to upgrade their communities' demographic profiles by discouraging prospective homebuyers of more modest means (disproportionately ethnic minorities) from living in the community.

The Impact of Regulatory Obstacles

In implementing these anti-growth strategies, many communities adopted such mechanisms as exclusionary zoning, impact fees, involuntary proffers, mandatory amenities, growth boundaries, service districts, infrastructure concurrency, and large-lot zoning. In the process, these regulations led to a significant escalation in home prices in target communities by limiting the supply of land for housing. These Smart Growth laws also contributed to suburban sprawl as modest-income families looked for less-expensive housing farther away from the metropolitan centers in communities that had yet to adopt Smart Growth prohibitions.

Despite the imposition of the many regulatory obstacles to buying homes in the suburbs, and despite efforts by the nation's aesthetic elites to demonize suburban living, the vast majority of American households opted to live in the suburbs instead of the more fashionable, albeit still dysfunctional, central cities or the older close-in suburbs. The latest U.S. Bureau of the Census population and migration figures indicate that this trend is continuing. Among the many reasons for this are the many benefits associated with owning a single-family detached house with some land, some equity, and some privacy, as well as the fact that Americans could buy "more house" if they were willing to move beyond the unaffordable, close-to-the-city communities.

Suburbanites also reaped the benefits of living in communities with functioning governments and quality public services, especially in education. While the commute to work was longer and the transportation costs greater, the several hundred thousand dollars in housing savings more than made up for the extra 20 or 30 minutes of additional driving time.

An Increase in Coercive Strategies

Recognizing that their anti-growth strategies have failed to deter the millions of American families that still flock to the burbs, Smart Growth advocates have now enlisted the federal government in their war against the suburbs, and the HUD-DOT partnership is the beginning of that effort. Although there is no shortage of detailed information from many sources (including HUD) on housing costs for every state, metropolitan area, and municipality in America, Smart Growth advocates contend that these readily available data are incorrect because they overlook the many "hidden costs" of suburban lifestyles, an assertion that relies on unsubstantiated allegations of greater infrastructure costs, environmental degradation, and the high cost of automobile operation.

Notwithstanding Smart Growth assertions to the contrary, public transit requires massive federal subsidies to maintain even its current mediocre and expensive service.

To save Americans from these alleged higher living costs, the Smart Growth and New Urbanist movements want Americans to move into higher-density developments—such as townhouses and high-rise apartment buildings—which, the anti-suburbanists contend, can be better served by public transportation (hence the commitment to "transportation choice," a process whereby commuters are bribed or coerced into an inconvenient mode of transportation that most would not choose on their own)—thereby freeing the hapless American people from relying on their automobiles. Other key benefits illuminated in this fable are the preservation of land, reduced carbon footprints, greater social interaction through forced proximity, and a higher aesthetic standard in community and housing design as government planners and politicians assume greater responsibility for artistic choices.

As with most other fables, the fundamental premise of the Smart Growth effort to restructure American lives rests on fabricated assumptions that have no support either in reality or in the copious housing and transportation data collected by the federal government and other institutions. As an earlier Heritage Foundation study using nationwide municipal data from the U.S. Bureau of the Census revealed, there is no evidence to indicate that infrastructure or other public costs in low-density suburbs are any greater than those in high-density communities.

The Real Cost of Public Transit

As for the alleged savings in transportation costs that are predicted to occur by shifting from cars to mass transit, data from a 2004 DOT study reveal that public transit survives on massive taxpayer subsidies that are generally hidden and excluded from any discussions of the relative costs and benefits of different modes of travel. When all costs are considered, public transit is far more expensive than automobiles.

That 2004 DOT study was expected to become an annual assessment, but congressional opposition to DOT's exposure of the high costs of urban transit and Amtrak forced DOT to cancel any subsequent studies. In response to President Obama's newest call for greater "transparency" in transportation costs, this DOT compilation of federal subsidies by transportation mode should be revived and made available to the public by Transportation Secretary Ray LaHood.

Recognizing the importance of accurate and up-to-date cost data in making good policy decisions, The Heritage Foundation has assumed responsibility for updating and maintaining this DOT series of federal subsidies by mode and will publish its findings this spring. Notwithstanding Smart Growth assertions to the contrary, public transit requires massive federal subsidies to maintain even its current mediocre and expensive service, which is used by less than 2 percent of the American population.

In 2006, the most recent period for which data are available, the federal subsidy for public transit amounted to $165.61 per 1,000 passenger miles, while automobiles earned the federal government a $0.93 "profit" per 1,000 passenger miles, in large part because federal fuel taxes paid by motorists are used to subsidize other projects, including transit. President Obama's commitment to transportation-cost "transparency" should include the compilation, calculation, and publication of this long-suppressed DOT data series.

Enhanced Central Planning by Government

Finally, the proposal exhibits a child-like faith in government planning, a concept that half the world quickly abandoned in the late 1980s when all of the formerly socialist countries (except, of course, for Cuba and North Korea) rejected state planning in favor of private-sector initiative, economic freedom, and market solutions. Nonetheless, and ever the optimist, the President proposes that the existing regional planning authorities be given yet more responsibility—and power.

At present, HUD requires states, counties, and cities to conduct five-year Consolidated Plans estimating housing status and needs, and DOT requires the federally funded Metropolitan Planning Organizations (MPOs) to develop Long-Range Transportation Plans and four-year Transportation Improvement Programs. Despite billions of dollars of spending on these entities, all of this costly planning coincided with what many believe has been one of the worst housing and transportation environments in U.S. history. Over the past decade, housing became less affordable than ever, and this has contributed to the most severe housing recession since the Great Depression. While all of the MPOs were huffing and puffing away on their little transportation plans, traffic congestion continued to worsen, and the quality of the transportation infrastructure continued to decline, despite record federal and state transportation spending on both.

Nonetheless, having failed separately to come anywhere close to performing the straightforward tasks assigned to them, the White House proposes that these two forms of planning initiatives be combined in a cooperative partnership, and that they be given even more responsibility and greater control over living and travel policies for the American people.

Organizations to Contact

The editors have compiled the following list of organizations concerned with the issues debated in this book. The descriptions are derived from materials provided by the organizations. All have publications or information available for interested readers. The list was compiled on the date of publication of the present volume; names, addresses, phone and fax numbers, and e-mail and Internet addresses may change. Be aware that many organizations take several weeks or longer to respond to inquiries, so allow as much time as possible.

American Farmland Trust (AFT)
1200 18th St. NW, Suite 800, Washington, DC   20036
(202) 331-7300 • fax: (202) 659-8339
e-mail: info@farmland.org
website: www.farmland.org

The American Farmland Trust (AFT) is a nonprofit membership organization founded in 1980 by a group of farmers and conservationists concerned about the rapid loss of the nation's farmland to development. AFT works with farmers and ranchers, political leaders, and community activists to protect agricultural resources. The group publishes a magazine called *American Farmland* and its website contains a wealth of information about the tensions between urban sprawl and farmland preservation.

Brookings Institution
1775 Massachusetts Ave. NW, Washington, DC   20036
(202) 797-6000
website: www.brookings.edu

The Brookings Institution is a nonprofit public policy organization that conducts independent research. The Brookings Institution's Metropolitan Policy Program was created in 1996 to provide policy makers with research and policy ideas for improving the health and prosperity of cities and metropolitan areas. The Brookings Institution publishes a variety of books, reports, and several journals, including the book *The Metropolitan Revolution: Building the Next Economy from the Ground Up.*

Congress for the New Urbanism (CNU)
The Marquette Bldg., 140 S. Dearborn St., Suite 404
Chicago, IL   60603
(312) 551-7300 • fax: (312) 346-3323
e-mail: cnuinfo@cnu.org
website: www.cnu.org

The Congress for the New Urbanism (CNU) is an organization that promotes walkable, mixed-use neighborhood development, sustainable communities, and healthier living conditions. CNU promotes these hallmarks of what it calls New Urbanism in communities across North America and overseas. CNU's website lists a number of reports and publications on these issues, as well as links to other groups involved with New Urbanism and other urban sprawl issues.

National Trust for Historic Preservation
1785 Massachusetts Ave. NW, Washington, DC   20036-2117
(800) 944-6847 • fax: (202) 588-6038
e-mail: info@nthp.org
website: www.preservationnation.org

The National Trust for Historic Preservation is a private, non-profit organization dedicated to saving historic places and revitalizing America's communities. The National Trust provides leadership, education, advocacy, and resources toward the goal of historic preservation. The organization has a variety of publications available at its website including the bimonthly magazine *Preservation.*

Natural Resources Defense Council (NRDC)
40 West 20th St., New York, NY   10011
(212) 727-2700 • fax: (212) 727-1773

e-mail: nrdcinfo@nrdc.org
website: www.nrdc.org

The Natural Resources Defense Council (NRDC) is an environmental action and membership organization that seeks to protect the planet's wildlife and wild places and to ensure a safe and healthy environment for all living things. One of NRDC's priority issues is fostering sustainable communities. NRDC's website contains information on smart growth, community planning, and information about its Smarter Cities project.

Sierra Club
85 Second St., 2nd Floor, San Francisco, CA   94105
(415) 977-5500 • fax: (415) 977-5797
e-mail: information@sierraclub.org
website: www.sierraclub.org

The Sierra Club is a membership organization working to protect communities, wild places, and the planet itself. The Sierra Club has developed a Climate Recovery Agenda—a set of initiatives aimed to cut carbon emissions 80 percent by 2050, reduce dependence on foreign oil, create a clean-energy economy, and protect the country from the consequences of global warming. The Sierra Club, through The Challenge to Sprawl Campaign, publishes numerous reports, factsheets, and articles on urban sprawl and new development.

Smart Growth America
1707 L St. NW, Suite 1050, Washington, DC   20036
(202) 207-3355
e-mail: info@smartgrowthusa.org
website: www.smartgrowthusa.org

Smart Growth America is a national organization dedicated to researching, advocating for, and leading coalitions to bring smart growth practices to more communities nationwide. Smart Growth America builds coalitions, develops policy, and conducts research toward that end. The organization publishes reports, available at its website, such as the recent "Building for the 21st Century: American Support for Sustainable Communities."

Smart Growth Network (SGN)
PO Box 3838, Butte, MT   59702
(866) 643-2767
e-mail: info@smartgrowth.org
website: www.smartgrowth.org

In 1996, the US Environmental Protection Agency joined with several nonprofit and government organizations to form the Smart Growth Network (SGN). SGN was formed in response to increasing community concerns about the need for new ways to grow that boost the economy, protect the environment, and enhance community vitality. SGN shares ideas for smart growth through its annual conference and through a variety of publications available at its website.

Trust for Public Land (TPL)
101 Montgomery St., Suite 900, San Francisco, CA   94104
(415) 495-4014
e-mail: info@tpl.org
website: www.tpl.org

The Trust for Public Land (TPL) is a nonprofit organization that conserves land for people to enjoy as parks, gardens, historic sites, rural lands, and other natural places. TPL helps communities plan for growth, raise funds, acquire land, and renovate parks and playgrounds, and it conducts conservation research. TPL publishes the biannual *Land&People* magazine and numerous books and reports.

United States Environmental Protection Agency (EPA)
Ariel Rios Bldg., 1200 Pennsylvania Ave. NW
Washington, DC   20460
(202) 272-0167
website: www.epa.gov

The United States Environmental Protection Agency (EPA) is a federal agency charged with protecting human health and the environment. The EPA writes regulations, sets national standards, and enforces regulations. The EPA's Office of Sustainable Communities publishes information on smart growth, available at its website.

Bibliography

Books

F. Kaid Benfield, Matthew D. Raimi, and Donald D.T. Chen
How Urban Sprawl Is Undermining America's Environment, Economy and Social Fabric. New York: Natural Resources Defense Council, 2001.

Basudeb Bhatta
Analysis of Urban Growth and Sprawl from Remote Sensing Data. New York: Springer, 2010.

Pamela Blais
Perverse Cities: Hidden Subsidies, Wonky Policy, and Urban Sprawl. Vancouver, British Columbia: UBC Press, 2010.

Robert Bruegmann
Sprawl: A Compact History. Chicago: University of Chicago Press, 2005.

Peter Calthorpe
Urbanism in the Age of Climate Change. Washington, DC: Island Press, 2011.

Wendell Cox
War on the Dream: How Anti-Sprawl Policy Threatens the Quality of Life. Lincoln, NE: iUniverse Books, 2006.

Andres Duany, Elizabeth Plater-Zyberk, and Jeff Speck
Suburban Nation: The Rise of Sprawl and the Decline of the American Dream. New York: North Point Press, 2010.

Dougla Farr
Sustainable Urbanism: Urban Design with Nature. Hoboken, NJ: Wiley, 2008.

John W. Frece — *Sprawl & Politics: The Inside Story of Smart Growth in Maryland.* Albany: State University of New York Press, 2008.

Edward L. Glaeser — *Triumph of the City: How Our Greatest Invention Makes Us Richer, Smarter, Greener, Healthier, and Happier.* New York: Penguin Press, 2011.

George A. Gonzalez — *Urban Sprawl, Global Warming, and the Empire of Capital.* Albany: State University of New York Press, 2009.

Claude Gruen — *New Urban Development: Looking Back to See Forward.* New Brunswick, NJ: Rutgers University Press, 2010.

H. Patricia Hynes and Russ Lopez, eds. — *Urban Health: Readings in the Social, Built, and Physical Environments of US Cities.* Sudbury, MA: Jones and Bartlett, 2009.

Char Miller, ed. — *Cities and Nature in the American West.* Reno: University of Nevada Press, 2010.

Randal O'Toole — *The Best-Laid Plans: How Government Planning Harms Your Quality of Life, Your Pocketbook, and Your Future.* Washington, DC: Cato Institute, 2007.

M. Paloma Pavel — *Breakthrough Communities: Sustainability and Justice in the Next American Metropolis.* Cambridge, MA: MIT Press, 2009.

Galina Tachieva	*Sprawl Repair Manual.* Washington, DC: Island Press, 2010.
Michael J. Thompson, ed.	*Fleeing the City: Studies in the Culture and Politics of Antiurbanism.* New York: Palgrave Macmillan, 2009.
Thad Williamson	*Sprawl, Justice, and Citizenship: The Civic Costs of the American Way of Life.* New York: Oxford University Press, 2010.
Jean-Marc Zaninetti	*Sustainable Development in the USA.* Hoboken, NJ: Wiley, 2009.

Periodicals and Internet Sources

Committee on Environmental Health, American Academy of Pediatrics	"The Built Environment: Designing Communities to Promote Physical Activity in Children," *Pediatrics*, vol. 123, no. 6, June 1, 2009.
Wendell Cox	"The Housing Crash and Smart Growth," *Policy Report No. 335*, National Center for Policy Analysis, June 2011. www.ncpa.org.
Wendell Cox and Ronald D. Utt	"Don't Regulate the Suburbs: America Needs a Housing Policy That Works," *Backgrounder*, March 5, 2009. www.heritage.org.
Jack Diamond	"Now Is the Time to Reshape Our Cities," *Globe & Mail* (Toronto, Canada), November 27, 2008.

William H. Frey   "The Demographic Lull Continues, Especially in Exurbia," Brookings Institution, April 6, 2012. www.brookings.edu.

Joseph Gidjunis   "Sprawl Exceeds Reach of Hydrants," *USA Today*, August 24, 2007.

Edward Glaeser   "Green Cities, Brown Suburbs," *City Journal*, Winter 2009.

David Gratzer   "The McVictim Syndrome Could Kill Us," *Los Angeles Times*, December 8, 2010.

Jesse A. Hamilton   "America's Future: The Heartland Versus the Coasts," *National Journal*, September 11, 2010. www.national journal.com.

Alyssa Katz   "The Reverse Commute," *American Prospect*, July/August 2010.

Bruce Katz   "Urbanization and Inventing a Clear Economy of Place," *Guardian* (UK), April 23, 2012.

Sam Kazman   "Oil Addiction," *American Spectator*, August 12, 2008.

Robert Kirkman   "Did Americans Choose Sprawl?" *Ethics & the Environment*, Spring 2010.

Joel Kotkin   "The War Against Suburbia," *American*, January 21, 2010. www.american.com.

Christopher B. Leinberger	"The Death of the Fringe Suburb," *New York Times*, November 25, 2011.
Alexis Madrigal	"The Beginning of the End for Suburban America," *Atlantic*, September 14, 2011. www.theatlantic .com.
John Bentley Mays	"Squeezed In, but Abounding in Open Space," *Globe & Mail* (Toronto, Canada), March 4, 2011.
Chelsea Murray	"Town and Country: Ontario's Greenbelt Saved 1.8 Million Acres of Green Space from Urban Sprawl. So Why Are the Farmers Who Live and Work There Moving Away?" *This Magazine*, July–August 2011.
Randal O'Toole	"Debunking Portland: The City That Doesn't Work," *Policy Analysis*, July 9, 2007. www.cato.org.
Witold Rybczynski	"Dense, Denser, Densest: Americans Like Their Cities Spacious. Will Concerns About Costs and the Environment Push Them to Rein in Sprawl?" *Wilson Quarterly*, Spring 2011.
Witold Rybczynski	"The Green Case for Cities," *Atlantic*, October 2009.
Jeffrey Simpson	"A Question of Sprawl: Live in the Past or Plan for the Future?" *Globe & Mail* (Toronto, Canada), June 9, 2009.

Chris Wolfe   "Steps to Solve L.A.'s Problems with
                       Traffic and Pollution," *Los Angeles
                       Business Journal*, April 2, 2007.

Ralph Zucker   "New Urbanism May Be Answer to
                       Garden State Housing," *Real Estate
                       Weekly*, April 11, 2007.

Index